AF507151

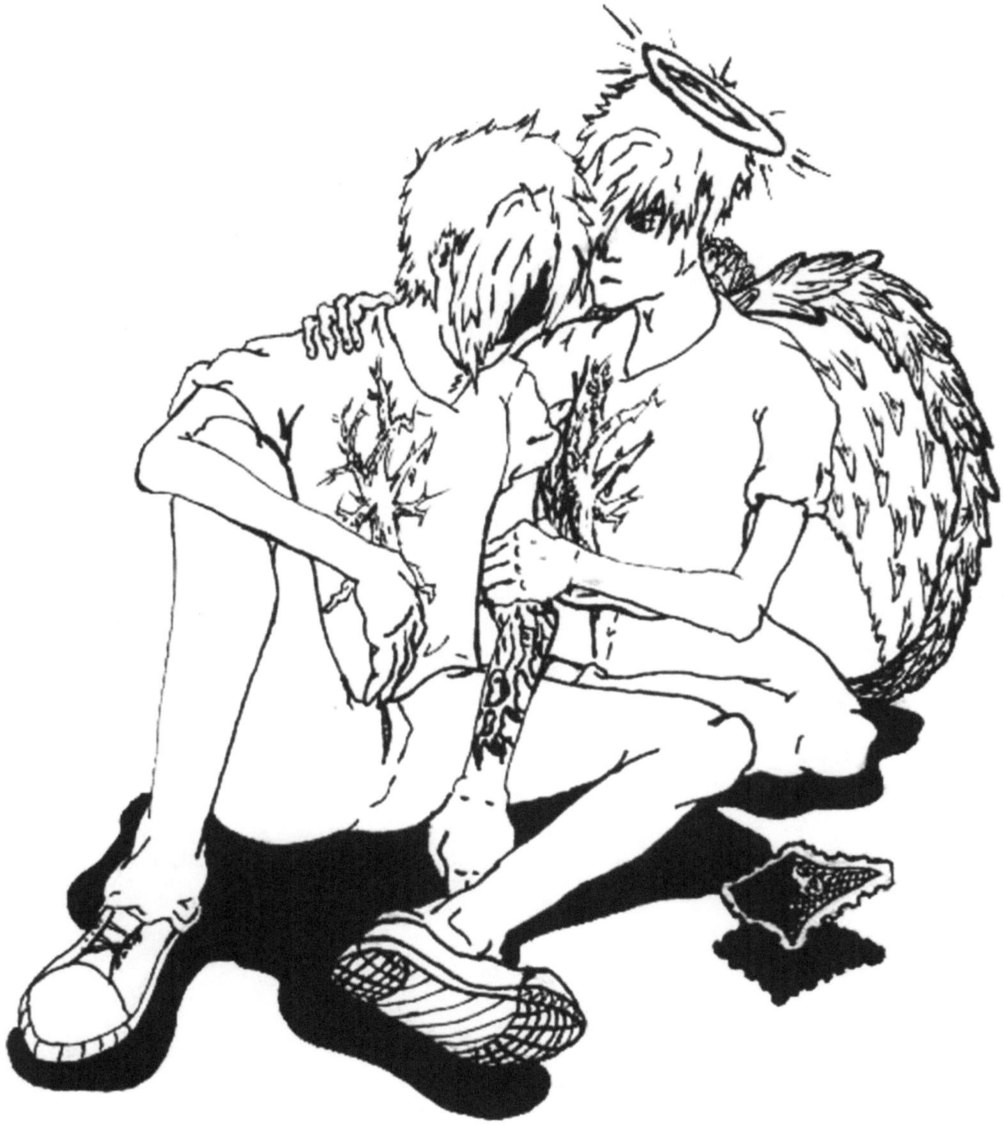

Inktober

2024

By
3ichael 7ambert

Michael Andrew Lambert Jr

Inktober is..

Inktober is an annual artistic challenge that invites creators from around the world to embrace the timeless beauty of ink. Originating in 2009, artist Jake Parker introduced this month-long event as a way to cultivate positive habits, improve drawing skills, and foster a global community of artists.

Throughout the month of October, participants, fondly known as "Inktoberists," embark on a creative journey by producing one ink-based artwork each day, guided by a set of daily prompts. These prompts are intentionally broad, allowing for a diverse range of interpretations and artistic styles.

Inktober not only serves as a platform for artists to showcase their talents but also fosters a sense of camaraderie within the creative community. Social media platforms come alive with a vibrant display of inked illustrations, providing a visual feast for art enthusiasts and aspiring creators alike.

Whether you are an established artist or a budding talent, Inktober stands as a testament to the power of daily artistic practice, the joy of experimentation, and the boundless possibilities that emerge when imagination meets ink.

So, dive into the enchanting world of ink, and let your creativity flow freely during this annual celebration of artistic expression.

Inktober List

DAY I	BACKBACK
DAY II	DISCOVER
DAY III	BOOTS
DAY IV	EXOTIC
DAY V	BINOCULARS
DAY VI	TREK
DAY VII	PASSPORT
DAY VIII	HIKE
DAY IX	SUN
DAY X	NOMADIC
DAY XI	SNACKS
DAY XII	REMOTE
DAY XIII	HORIZON
DAY XIV	ROAM
DAY XV	GUIDEBOOK
DAY XVI	GRUNGY
DAY XVII	JOURNAL
DAY XVIII	DRIVE
DAY XIX	RIDGE
DAY XX	UNCHARTED
DAY XXI	RHINOCEROS
DAY XXII	CAMP
DAY XXIII	RUST
DAY XXIV	EXPEDITION
DAY XXV	SCARECROW
DAY XXVI	CAMERA
DAY XXVII	ROAD
DAY XXVIII	JUMBO
DAY XXIX	NAVIGATOR
DAY XXX	VIOLIN
DAY XXXI	LANDMARK

In the realm of artistic expression, the choice of medium becomes a deeply personal decision, shaping the very essence of the creative journey. For this collection, I deliberately opted for the humble ballpoint pen—a seemingly mundane tool with an extraordinary capacity for nuance and subtlety.

The ballpoint pen, often overlooked in the realm of traditional art, becomes my steadfast companion throughout this Inktober odyssey. Its indomitable ink flow dances across the pages, unfurling a tapestry of lines and shades that bear witness to moments of inspiration and introspection.

While some may argue that ballpoint pens lack the finesse of other art supplies, it is precisely their inherent imperfections that drew me in. Each stroke tells a story of resilience, embracing smudges and uneven lines as the fingerprints of a creative journey. In the pages that follow, you'll encounter a spectrum of outcomes—some pieces are fully realized, while others stand as raw snapshots of a day's work, waiting to be expanded upon in the future. This collection is not about perfection but about the commitment to creation, even when the vision remains unfinished.

Within these inked pages, I invite you to explore the dichotomy of the imperfect and the proud. As I present this collection, I find pride not only in the meticulously crafted pieces but also in the moments where the pen danced freely, leaving behind traces of raw, unfiltered creativity.

So, let us celebrate the unpredictable beauty of ballpoint pen art—a medium that whispers tales of daring exploration, steadfast dedication, and the unapologetic embrace of imperfection. Some of these works may evolve beyond what you see here, but for now, they stand as the finished products of their respective days—a testament to the spirit of Inktober itself.

— Michael A. Lambert Jr.

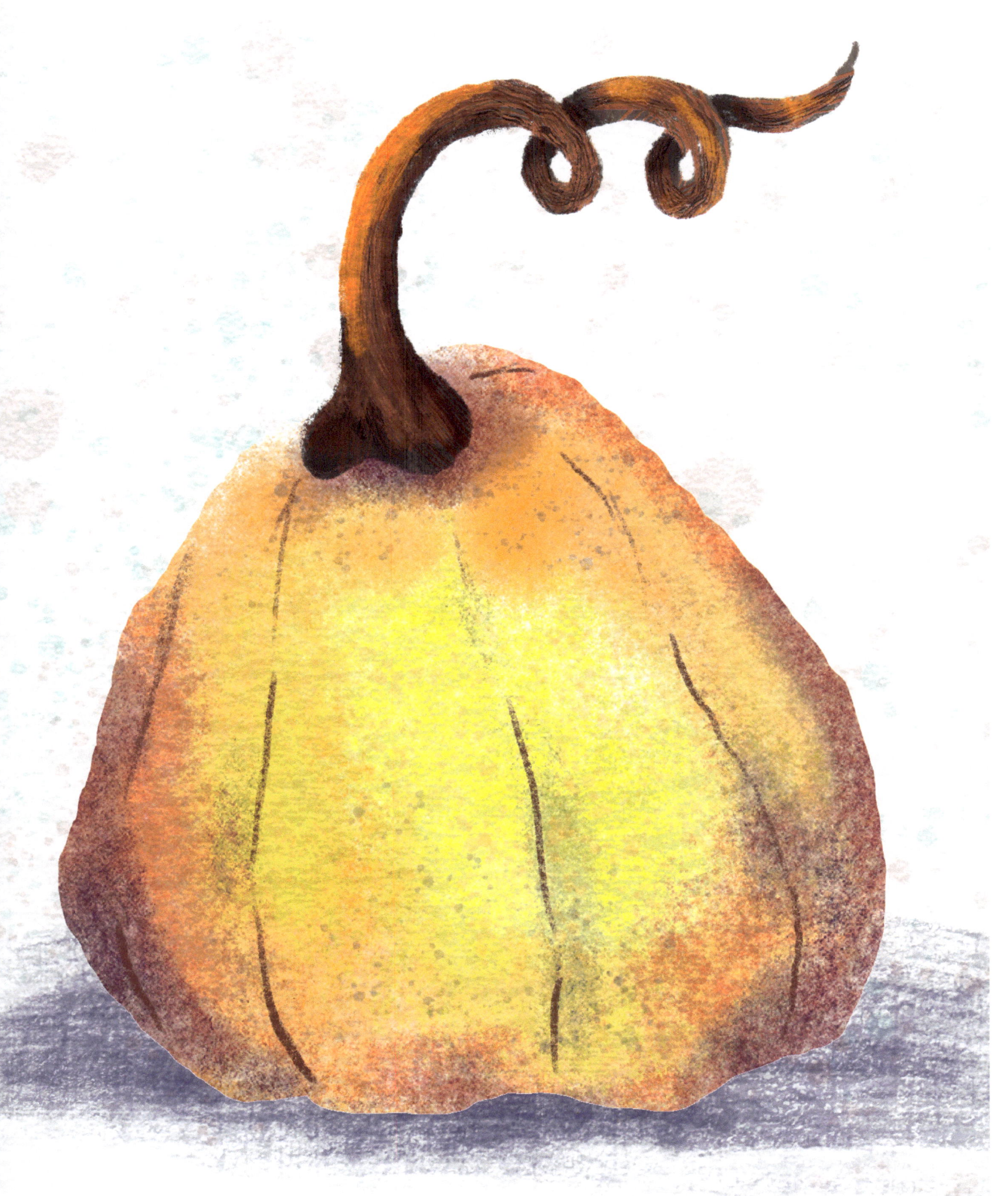

DAY I
BACKPACK

For Day 1, I kept it straightforward with a simple drawing of a backpack. There's nothing overly complex here—just the essential lines and shapes to bring the subject to life. It's a fitting start to the journey, symbolizing the tools and preparation needed to take on the creative challenges ahead.

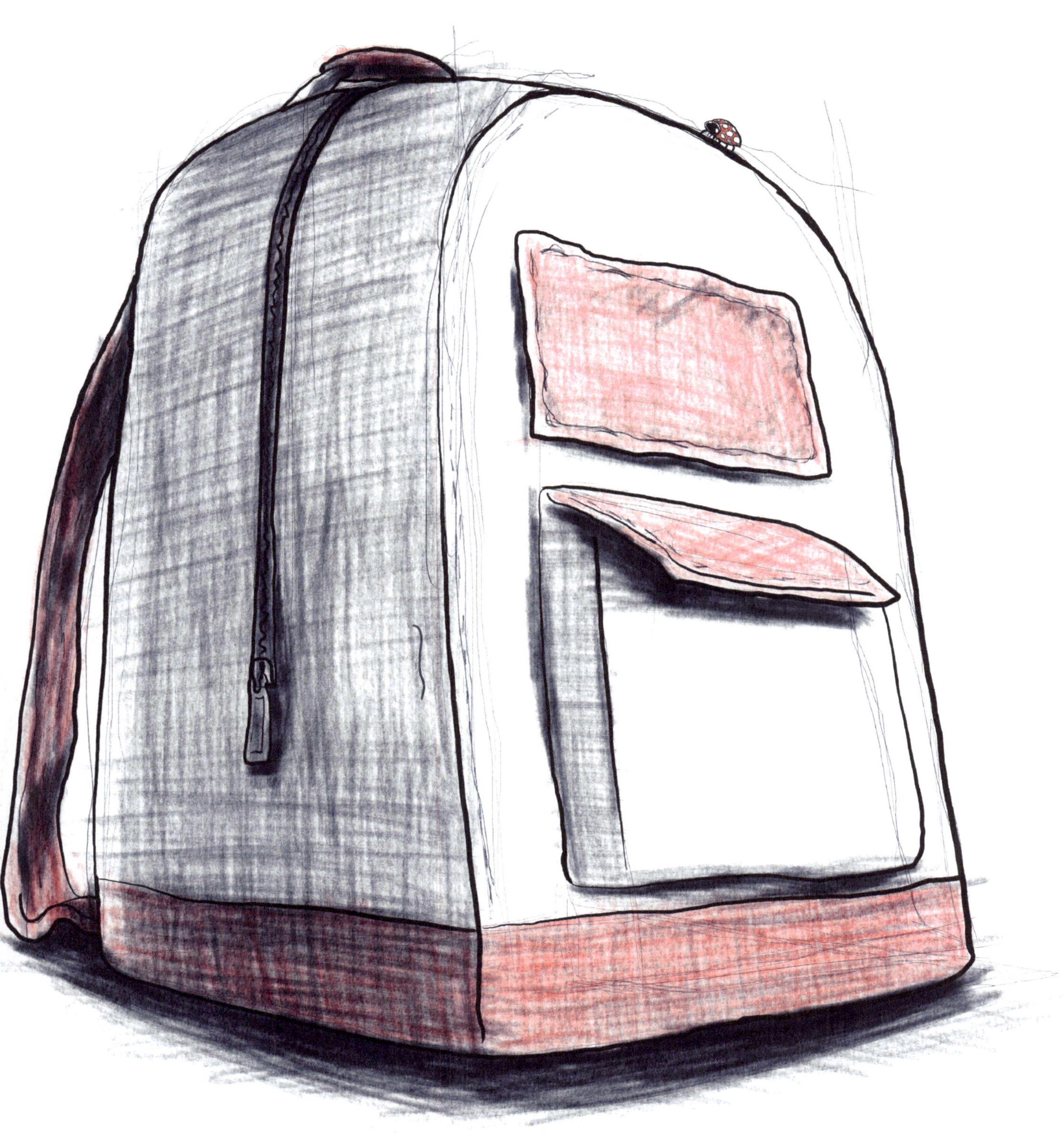

DAY II
DISCOVER

For Day 2, I set sail into the unknown with a drawing of a 1600s-style sailing ship, reminiscent of the vessels that once charted uncharted waters. The towering masts, billowing sails, and intricate rigging capture a spirit of adventure and exploration. This piece embodies the theme of discovery—not just of distant lands, but of creativity itself. Each stroke of the pen, like the wind in a ship's sails, propels this artistic journey forward into new and uncharted territory.

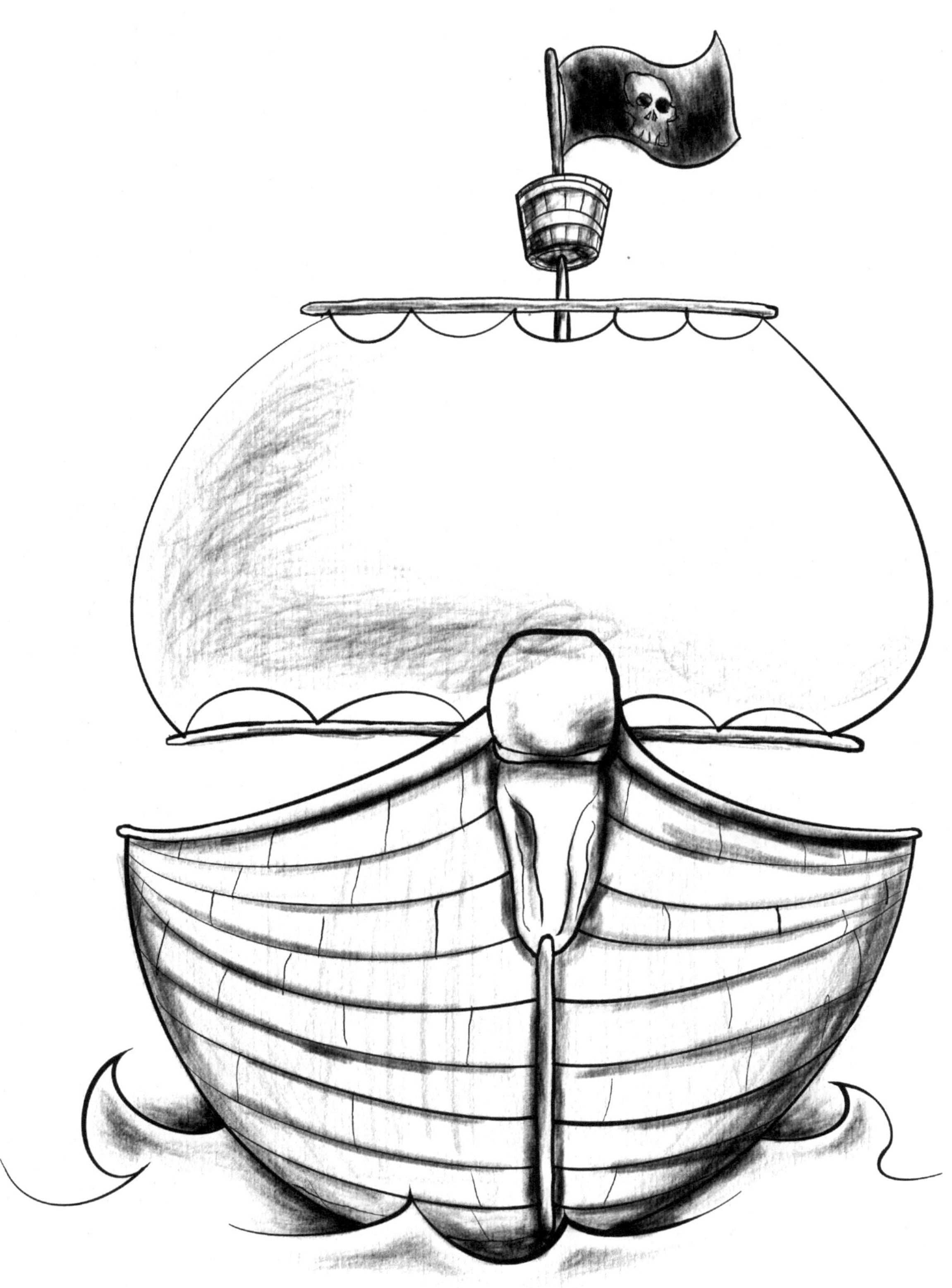

DAY III
BOOTS

For Day 3, I focused on a sturdy, well-worn work boot—
a symbol of resilience, hard work, and the paths we
walk in life. The thick soles and rugged leather tell a
story of perseverance, whether on job sites, long treks,
or personal journeys. With each pen stroke, I aimed to
capture the texture and weight of something built to
endure. Just like the creative process, a good pair of
boots carries you forward, step by step.

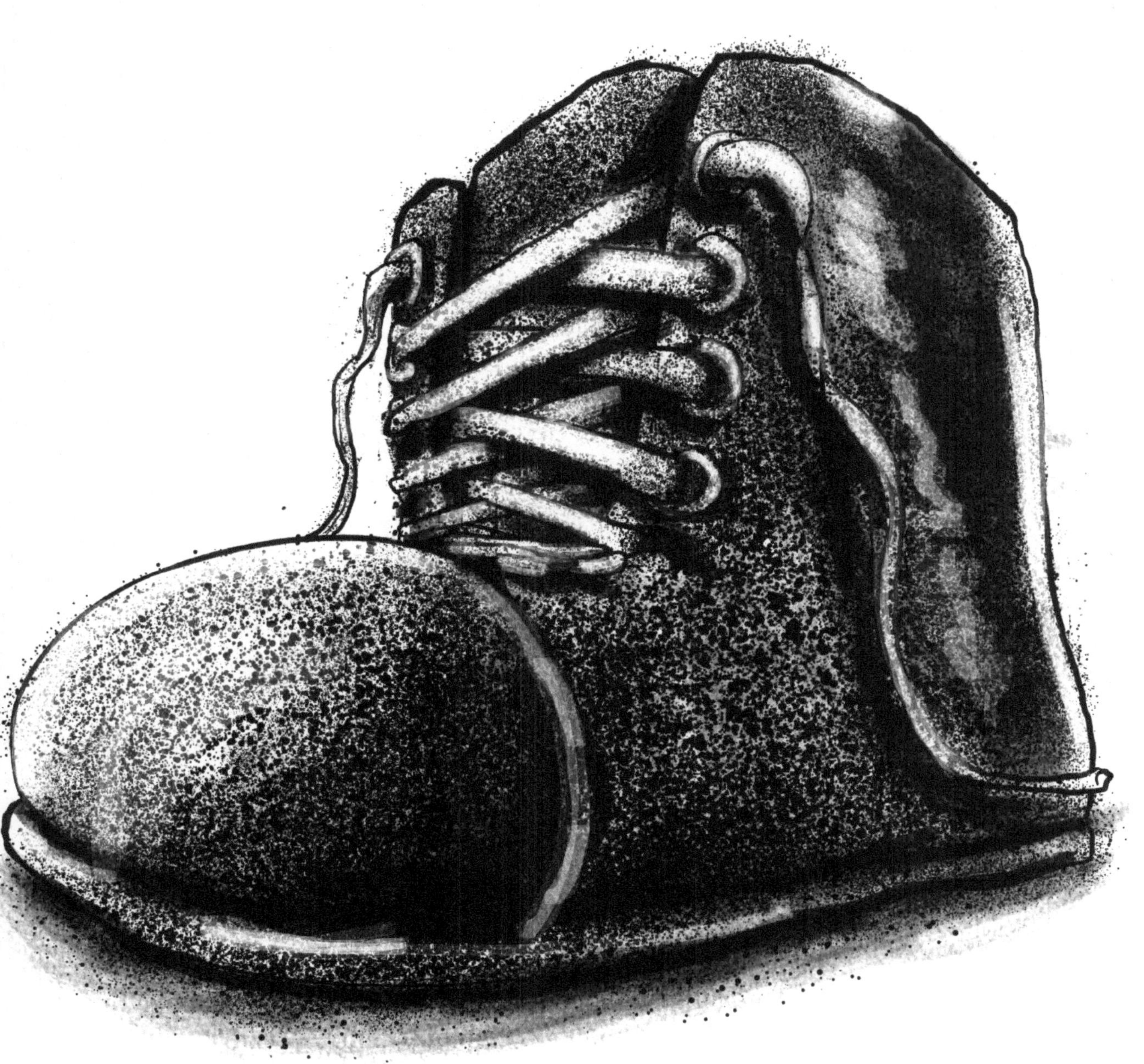

DAY IV
EXOTIC

For Day 4, I explored something both delicate and eerie —the skeletal remains of a bird. Bones tell their own story, revealing the structure beneath what was once vibrant and alive. There's something exotic about what lies beneath, a hidden framework that supports flight and freedom. With each fine pen stroke, I traced the fragile architecture of hollow bones, capturing the beauty in what is often unseen. In its stillness, the skeleton holds a quiet mystery—an echo of movement, migration, and the passage of time.

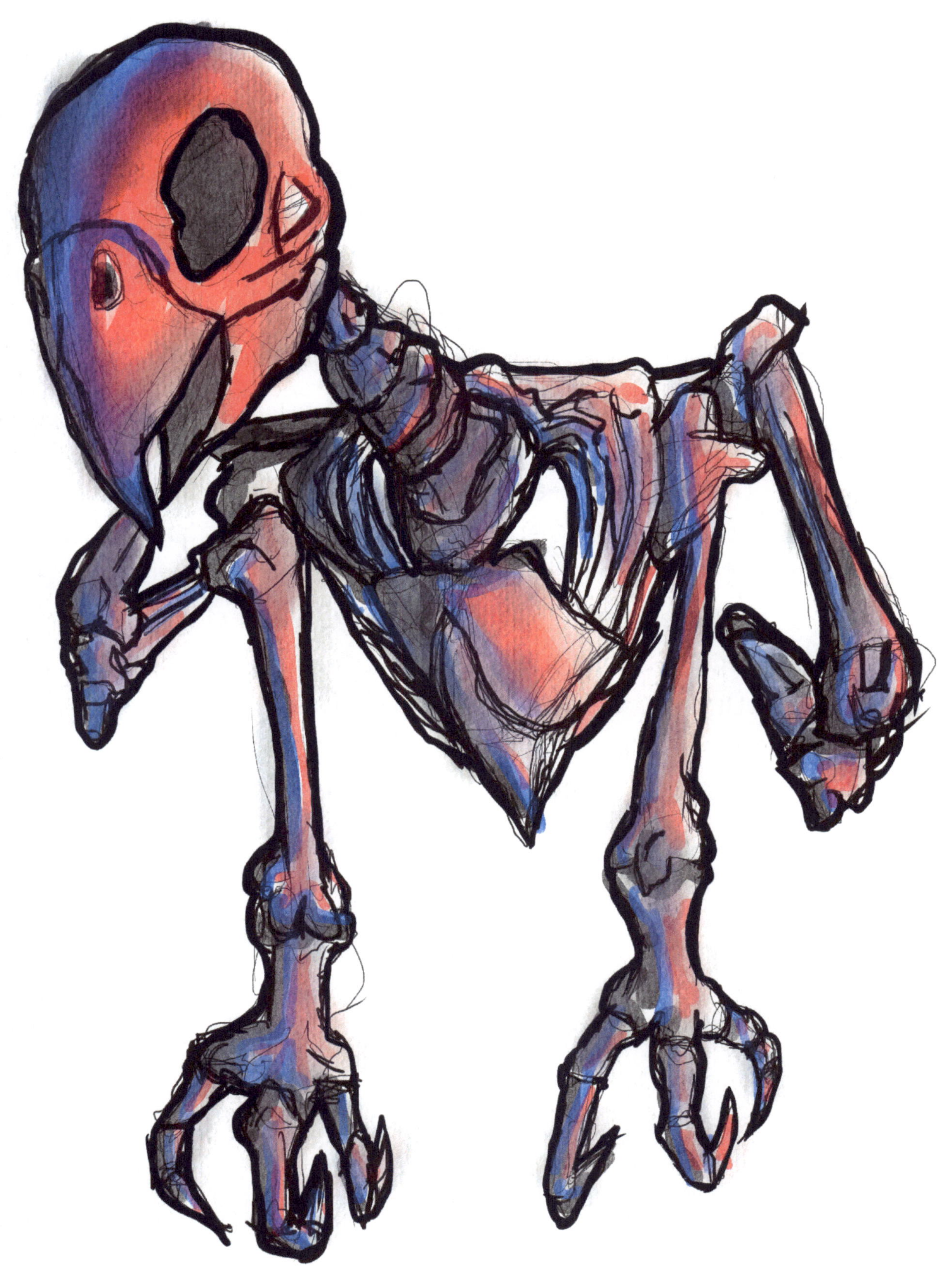

DAY V
BINOCULARS

For Day 5, I began exploring perspective by drawing a close-up, extreme-angle view of a boy holding binoculars. The exaggerated foreshortening pulls the viewer into the scene, as if looking directly through the lenses themselves. This piece plays with depth and scale, emphasizing the way binoculars distort and expand our field of vision. Just as they bring distant things closer, this drawing challenges perception, drawing focus to the unseen details hiding in plain sight.

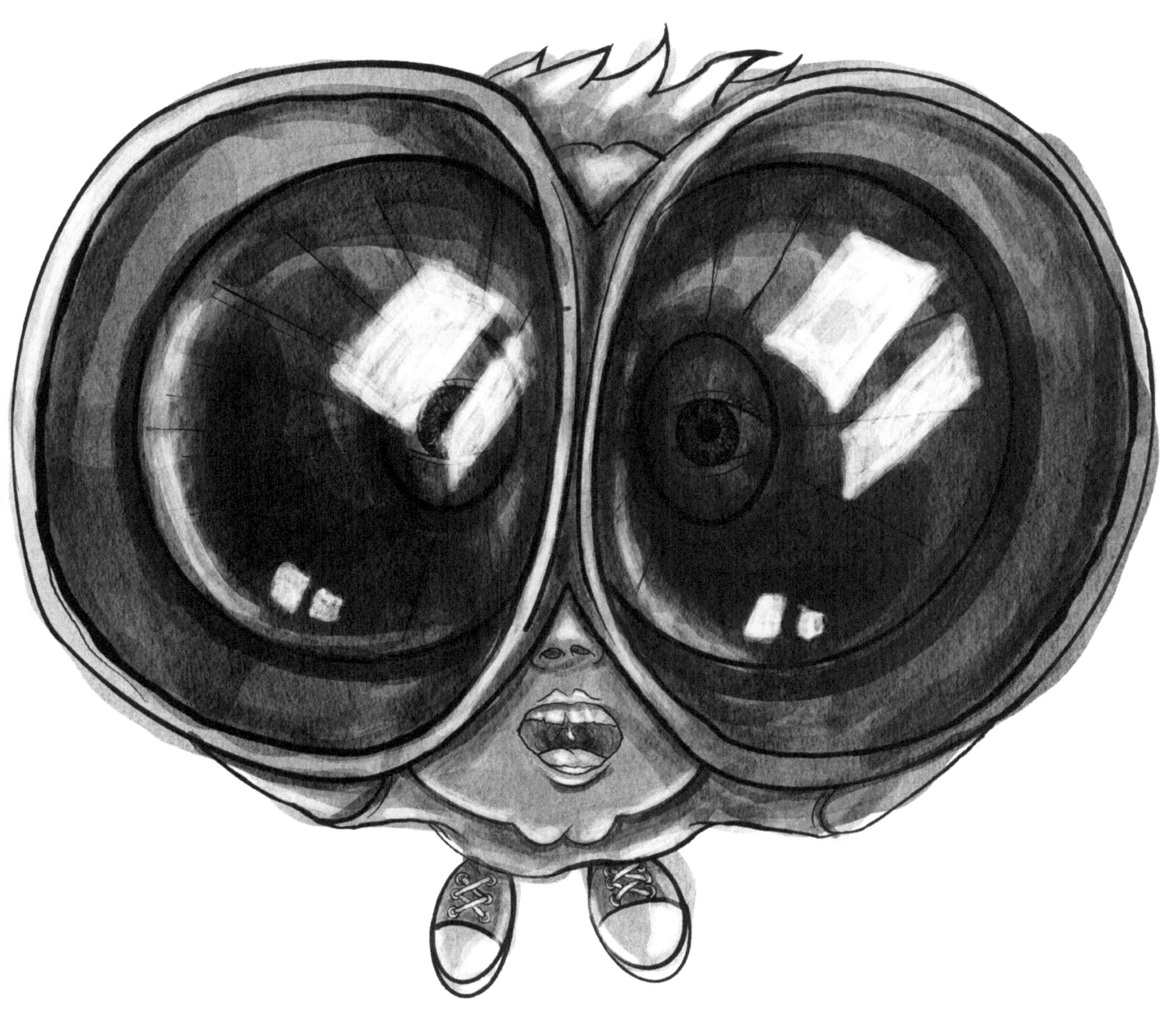

DAY VI
TREK

For Day 6, I fully embraced perspective as my theme, illustrating a cyclist on a path beside Sloan's Lake, with the Denver skyline rising across the water. The piece captures a dramatic 5-point "little planet" perspective, curving the world into a spherical view that immerses the viewer in the scene. The cyclist's trek becomes symbolic of movement, exploration, and the interconnectedness of urban life and nature. This drawing marks a turning point in my Inktober journey, where perspective took center stage, transforming each piece into a study of depth, angles, and the boundless potential of ballpoint pen art and alcohol markers.

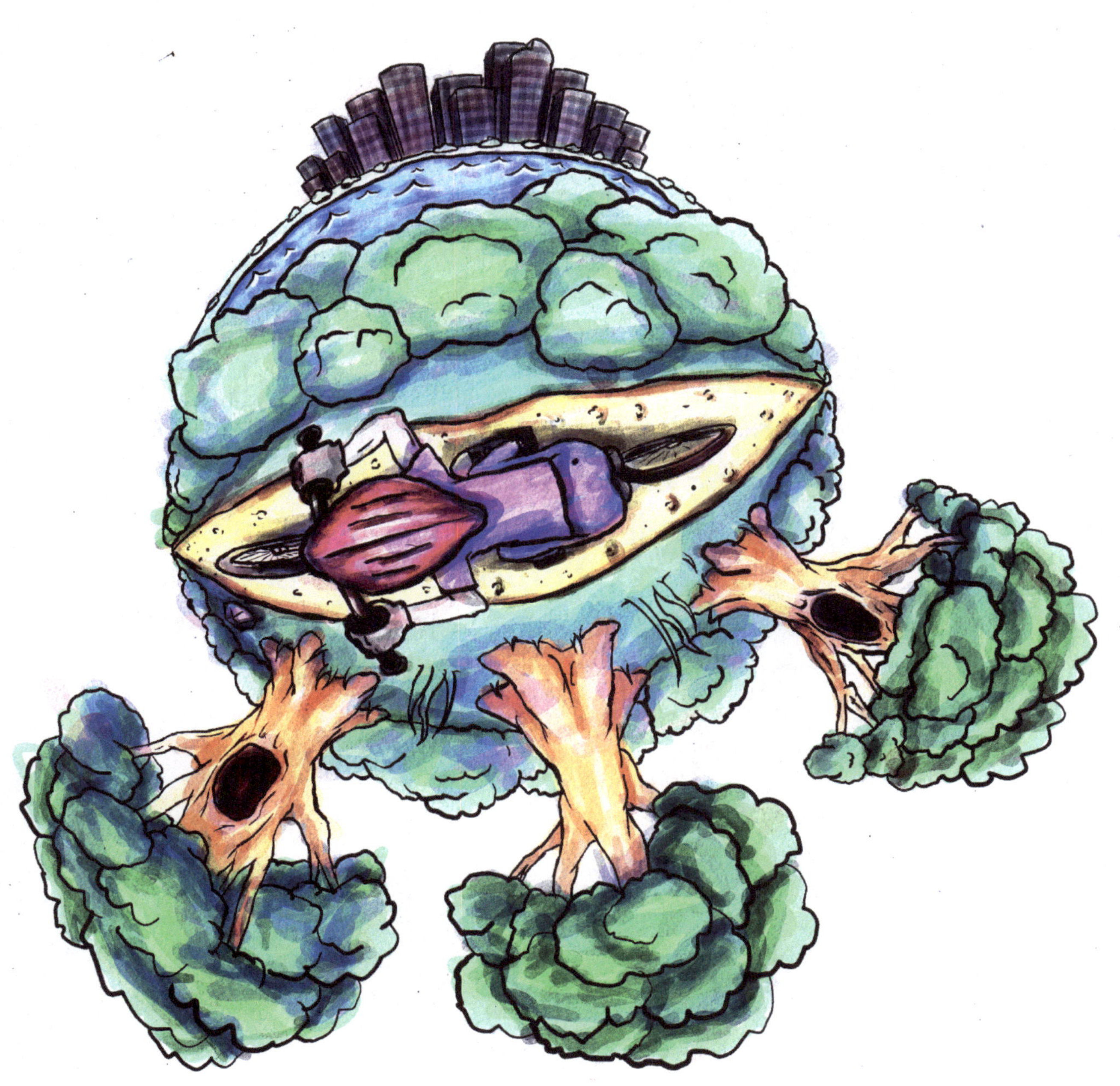

DAY VII
PASSPORT

For Day 7, I continued my exploration of 5-point "little planet" perspective, this time creating a world filled with iconic landmarks. Big Ben, the Eiffel Tower, the Great Wall of China, the Pyramids, and Stonehenge all curve around the spherical landscape, forming a surreal, globe-spanning composition. This piece embodies the spirit of travel and discovery—the way a passport grants access to different cultures, histories, and architectural wonders. Through ballpoint pen and alcohol markers, I aimed to capture the thrill of seeing the world in a single frame, where borders blur and every destination exists within reach.

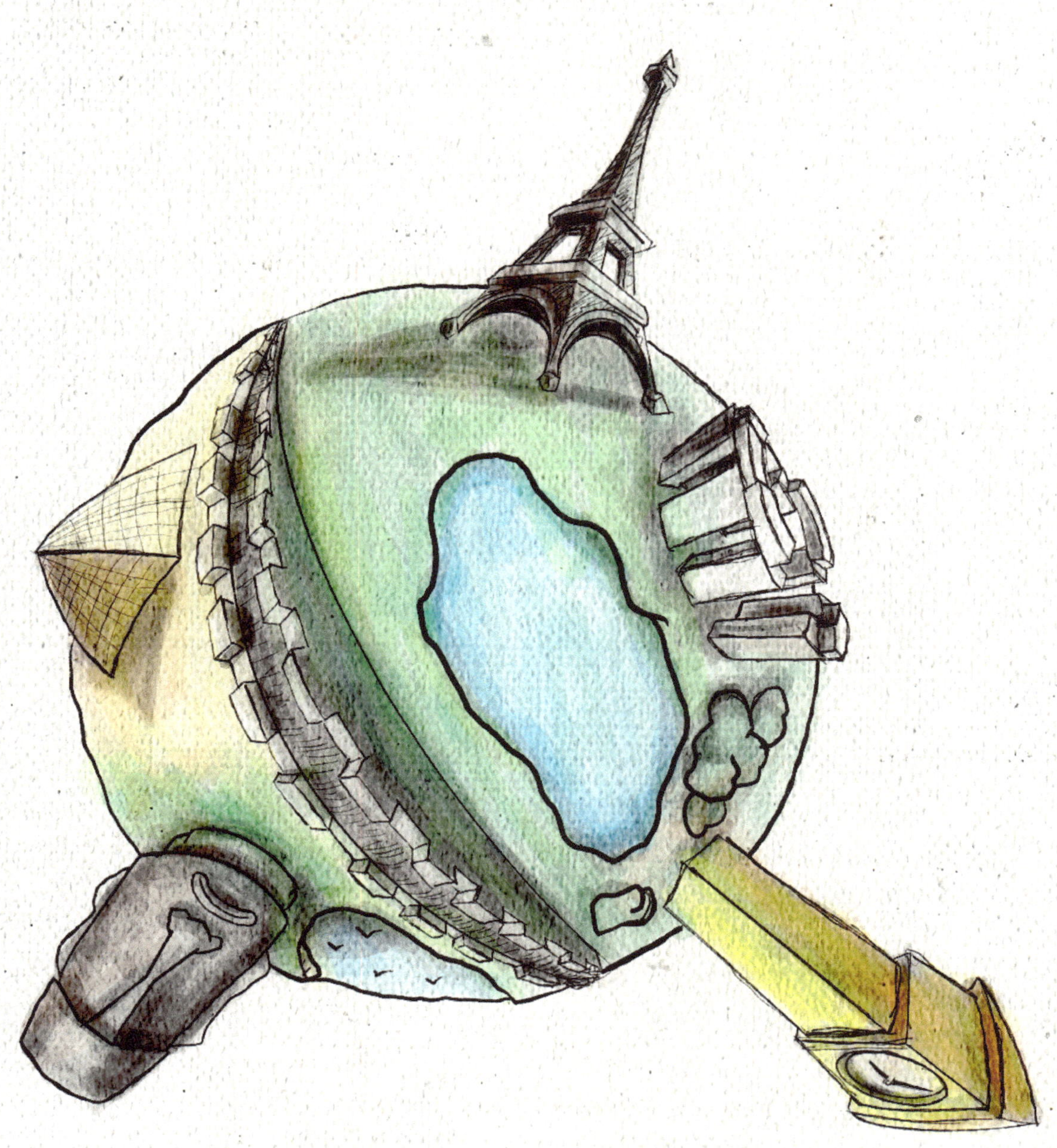

DAY VIII
BACKPACK

For Day 8, I flipped my approach to perspective, creating an inverted 5-point "rabbit hole" view. Instead of a world curving outward, this piece pulls the viewer inward—down a spiraling forest landscape with towering trees, dense bushes, winding trails, and distant mountains. The scene invites a sense of adventure, as if stepping into the unknown with only a backpack and curiosity to guide the way. This drawing plays with depth and distortion, reinforcing the theme of exploration—both in nature and in artistic technique.

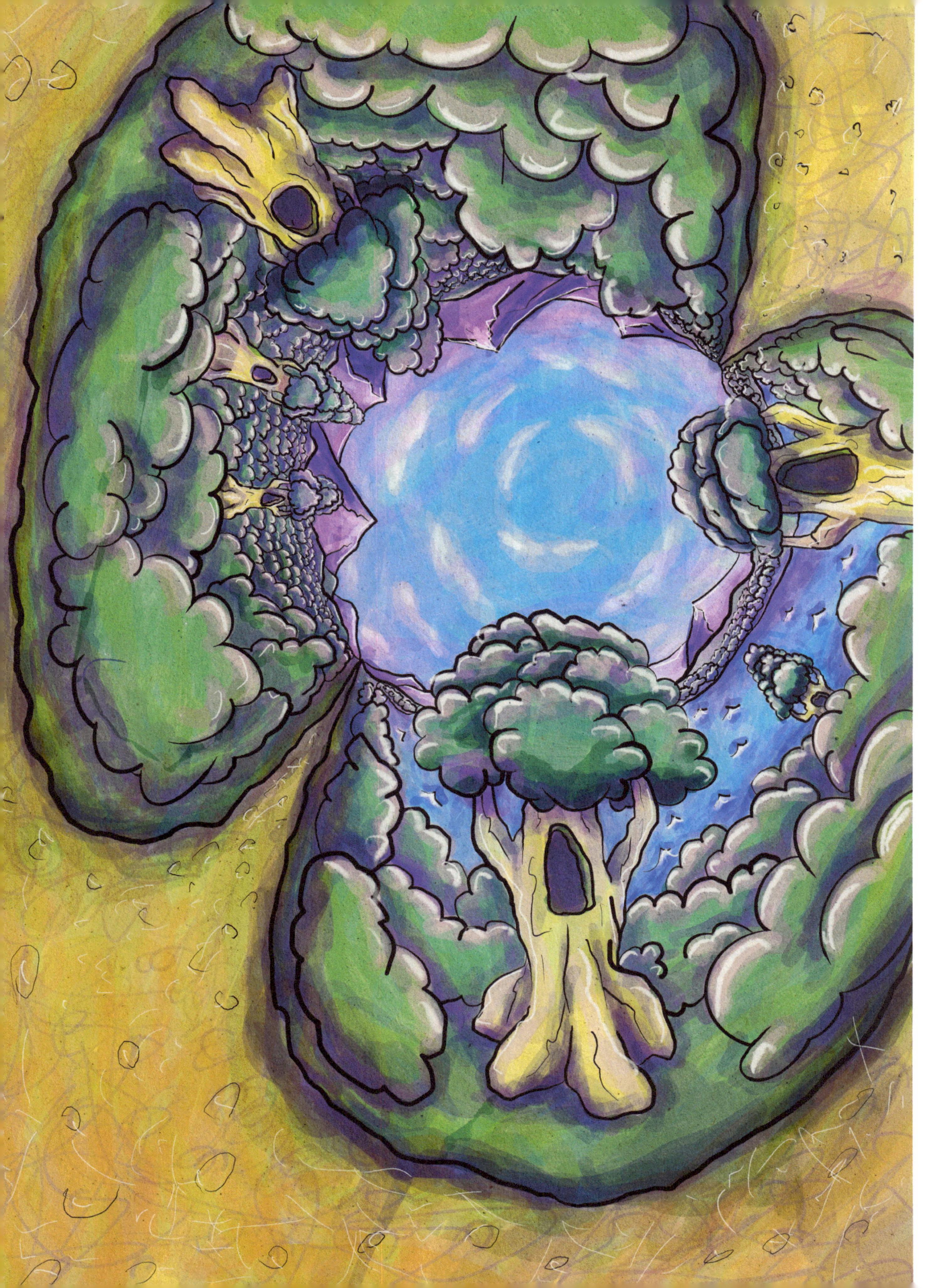

DAY IX
SUN

For Day 9, I shifted to a more structured approach, drawing a sun temple in 2-point perspective. The sharp lines and geometric precision give the structure a sense of grandeur and symmetry, evoking ancient civilizations that worshipped the sun as a source of power and life. This piece contrasts with my previous curved-perspective works, grounding the composition in architectural form while still playing with depth and scale. The temple stands as a tribute to light, energy, and the enduring influence of perspective in both art and history.

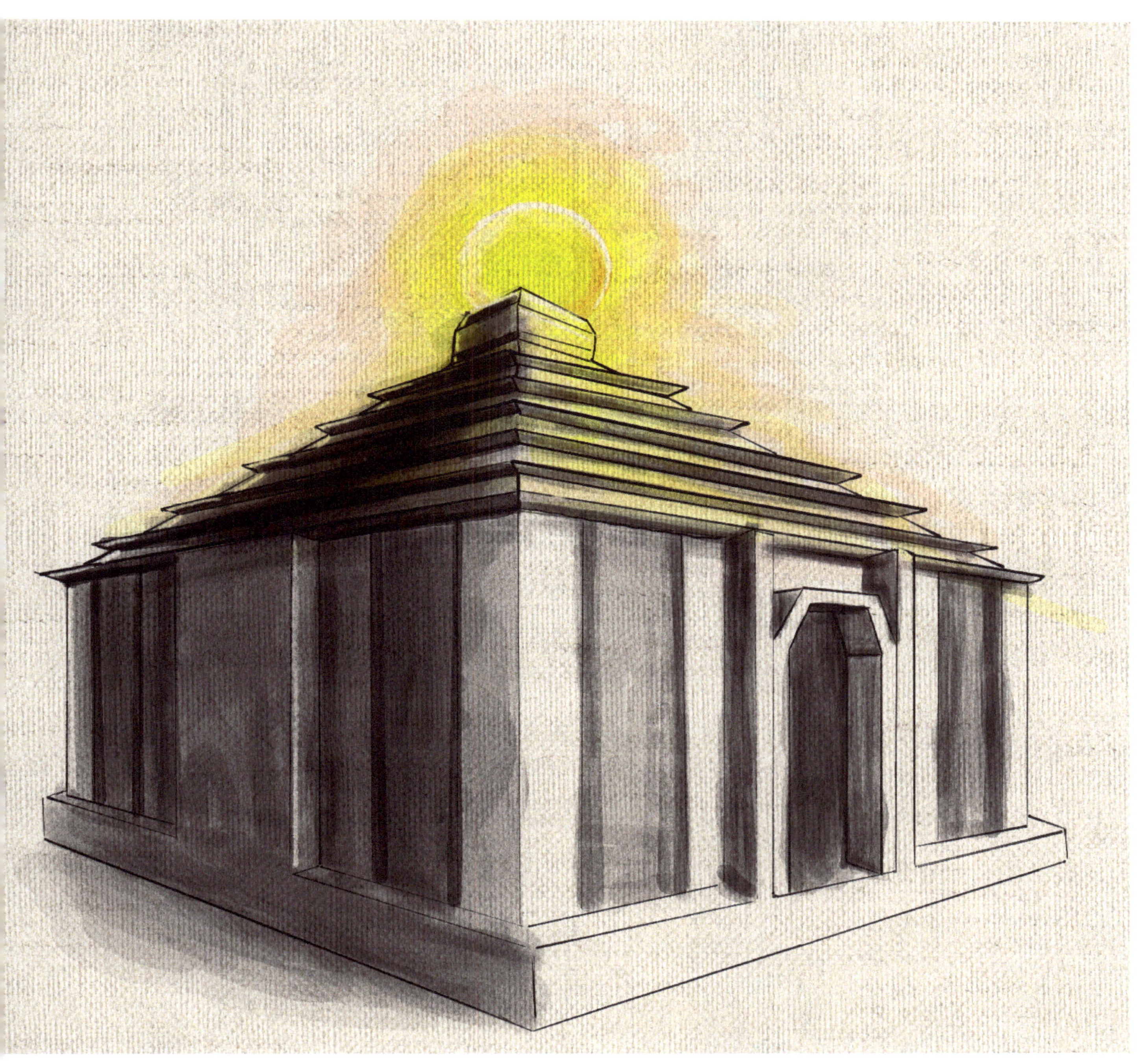

DAY X
NOMADIC

For Day 10, I returned to the rabbit hole 5-point perspective, this time immersing the viewer in the vastness of the Sahara Desert. A lone camel treks through the dunes, framed by the towering pyramids in the distance, their forms bending and warping within the surreal perspective. The circular composition enhances the sense of movement and isolation, capturing the essence of the nomadic spirit—endless horizons, uncharted paths, and the resilience to journey forward. I'm especially proud of how this piece came together compositionally, balancing depth, atmosphere, and the quiet grandeur of desert travel.

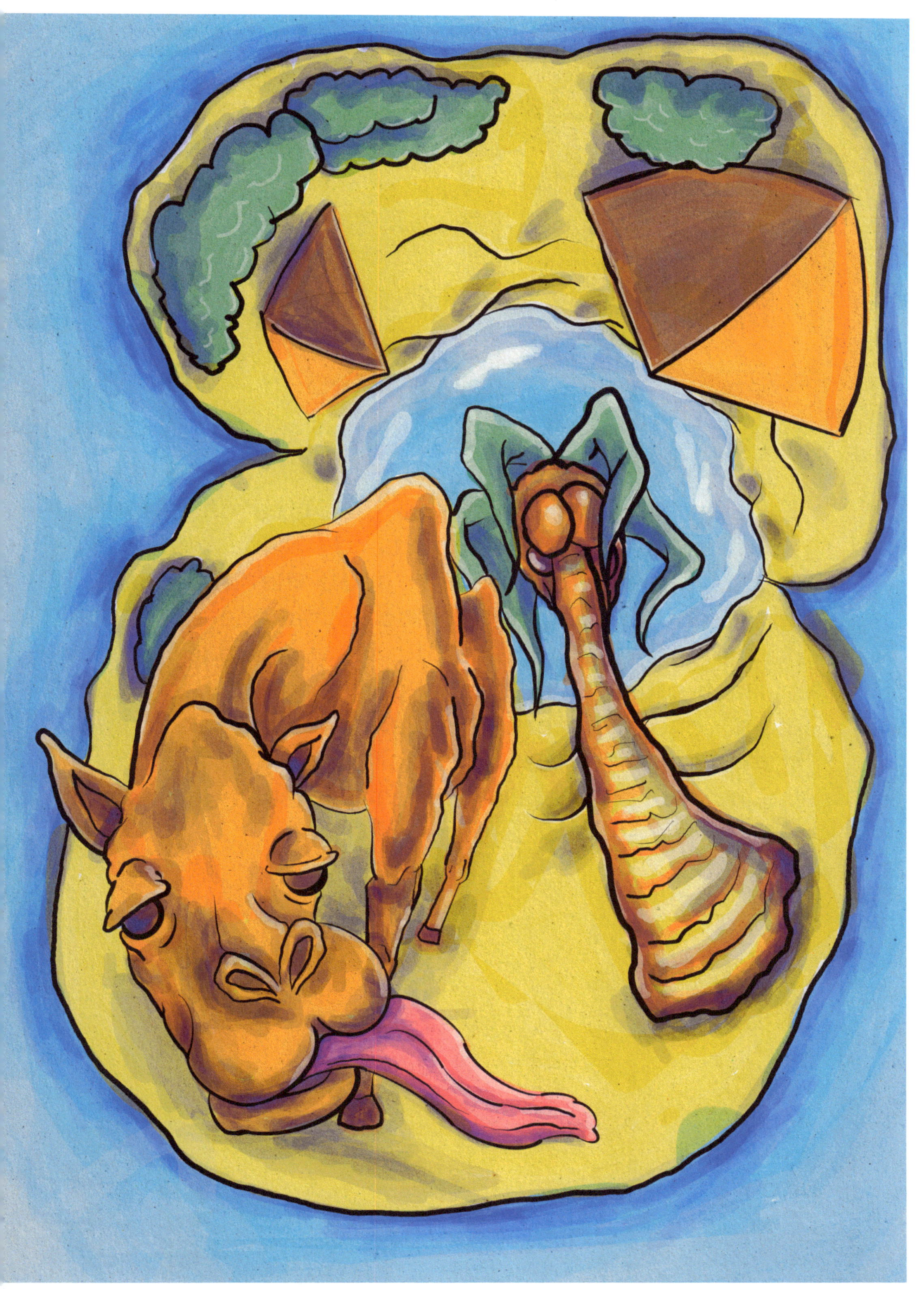

DAY XI
SNACKS

For Day 11, I took a whimsical turn, creating a rabbit hole 5-point perspective of a candy-filled world. The landscape twists and spirals into a vibrant, surreal Candy Land, with a giant lollipop as the focal point. The exaggerated depth and curving forms make the scene feel like a sugar-fueled dream, pulling the viewer deeper into a world of sweets. This piece was a fun departure from my previous works, blending playful imagination with intricate perspective to create a visually immersive experience.

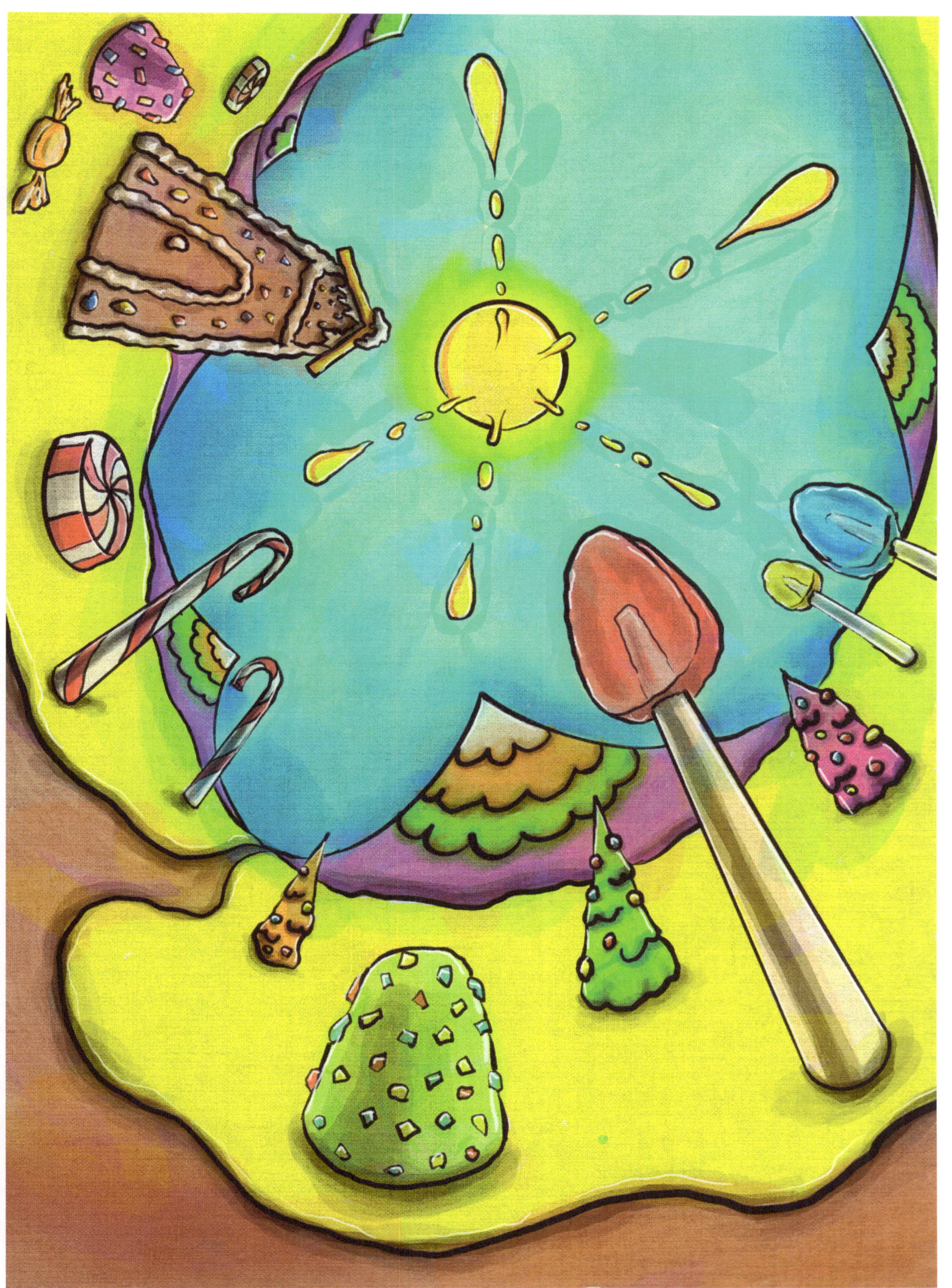

DAY XII
REMOTE

For Day 12, I explored a fisheye perspective, distorting the familiar form of a laptop into a dynamic, curved composition. The exaggerated proportions give the screen and keyboard a surreal depth, emphasizing the way technology connects us to the world no matter where we are. This piece plays with the concept of "remote" work, communication, and digital presence— how a single device can serve as a portal to endless possibilities. The fisheye effect adds an immersive quality, pulling the viewer into the digital space while reinforcing my ongoing study of perspective.

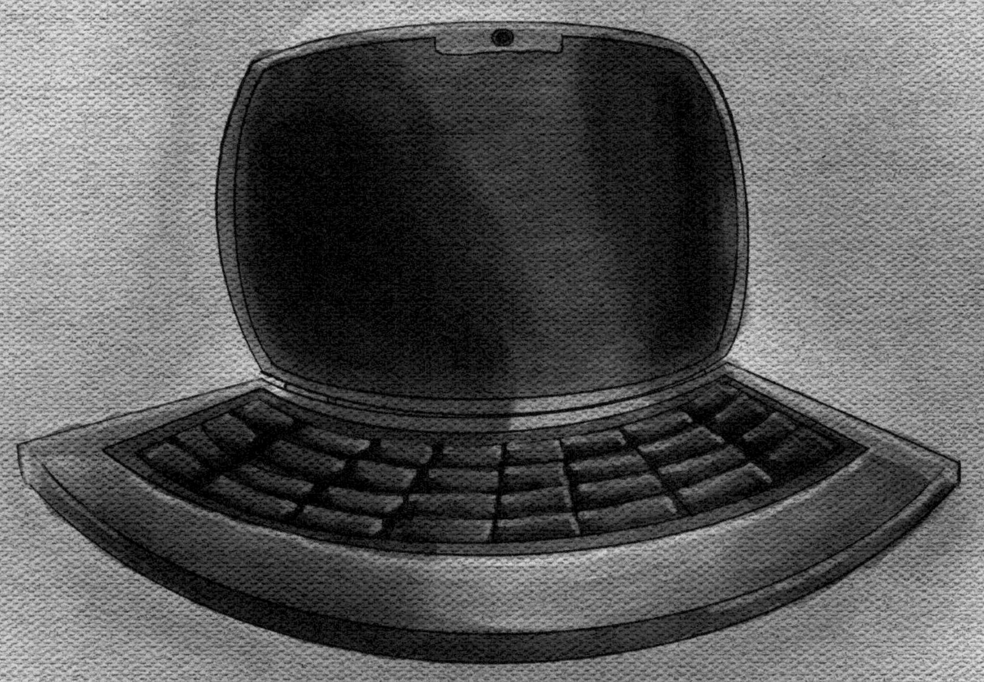

DAY XIII
HORIZON

For Day 13, I experimented with dual 5-point perspectives, aiming to create a full 360-degree view of space—capturing both the front and back of the scene simultaneously. The composition features asteroids drifting between the Sun and Moon, attempting to blend two vanishing points into a single immersive perspective. While the concept was ambitious, the lack of depth made it a challenge to fully achieve the intended effect. Still, this piece serves as a valuable exploration of spatial perception, pushing the boundaries of how perspective can be applied beyond traditional landscapes.

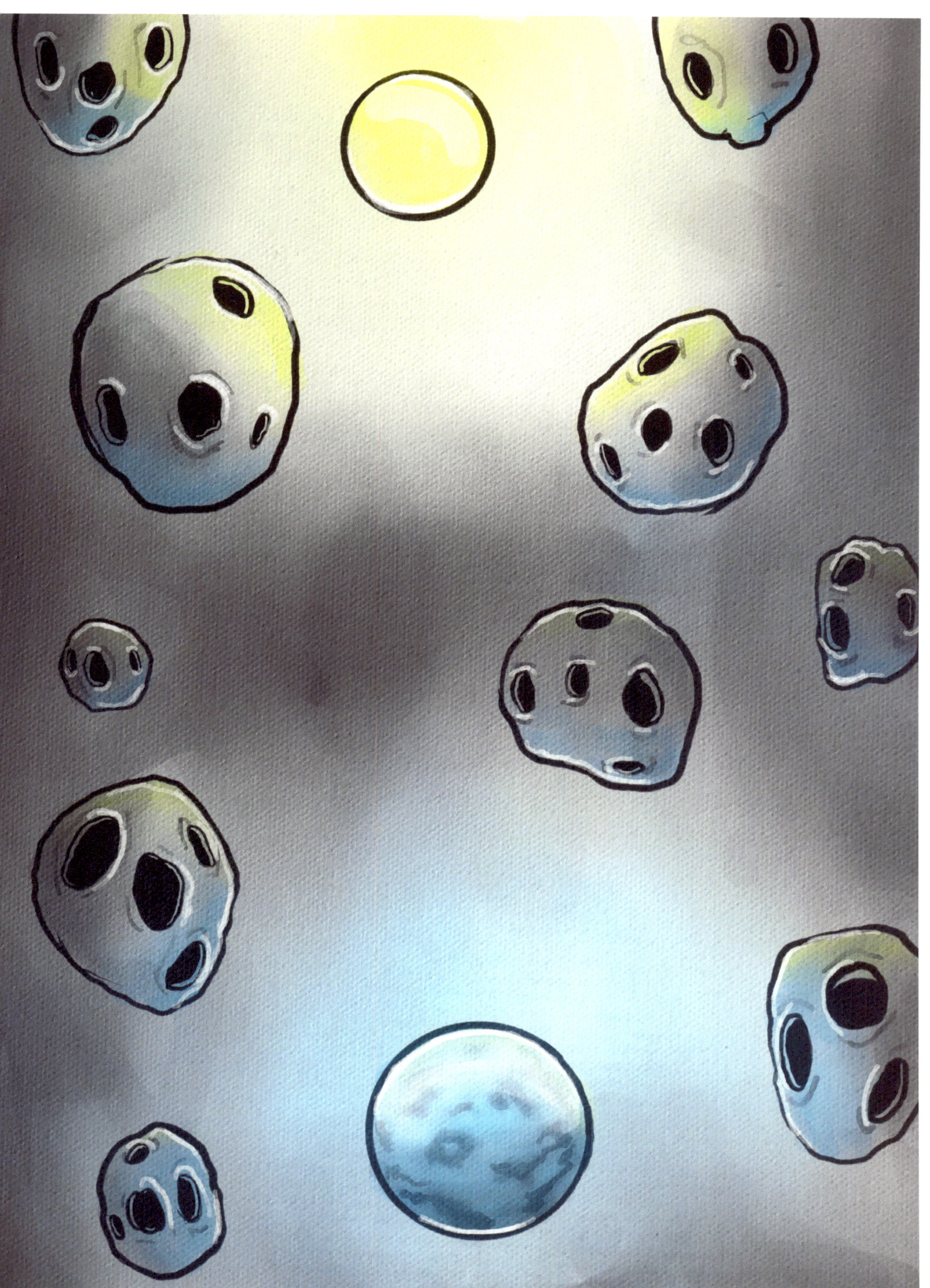

DAY XIV
ROAM

As a continuation of my Day 10 camel piece, I explored a Western-inspired variant for Day 14—this time featuring a lone horse against a dramatic red sky stretching from Arizona to Texas. Using my signature 5-point perspective, I aimed to capture the vastness of the open desert, where the horizon feels endless and the landscape tells stories of movement and solitude. The bold sky and rugged terrain enhance the sense of freedom, reinforcing the untamed spirit of the West. This piece builds on the nomadic theme, shifting from the Sahara to the American frontier, where both creatures roam vast lands shaped by time and nature.

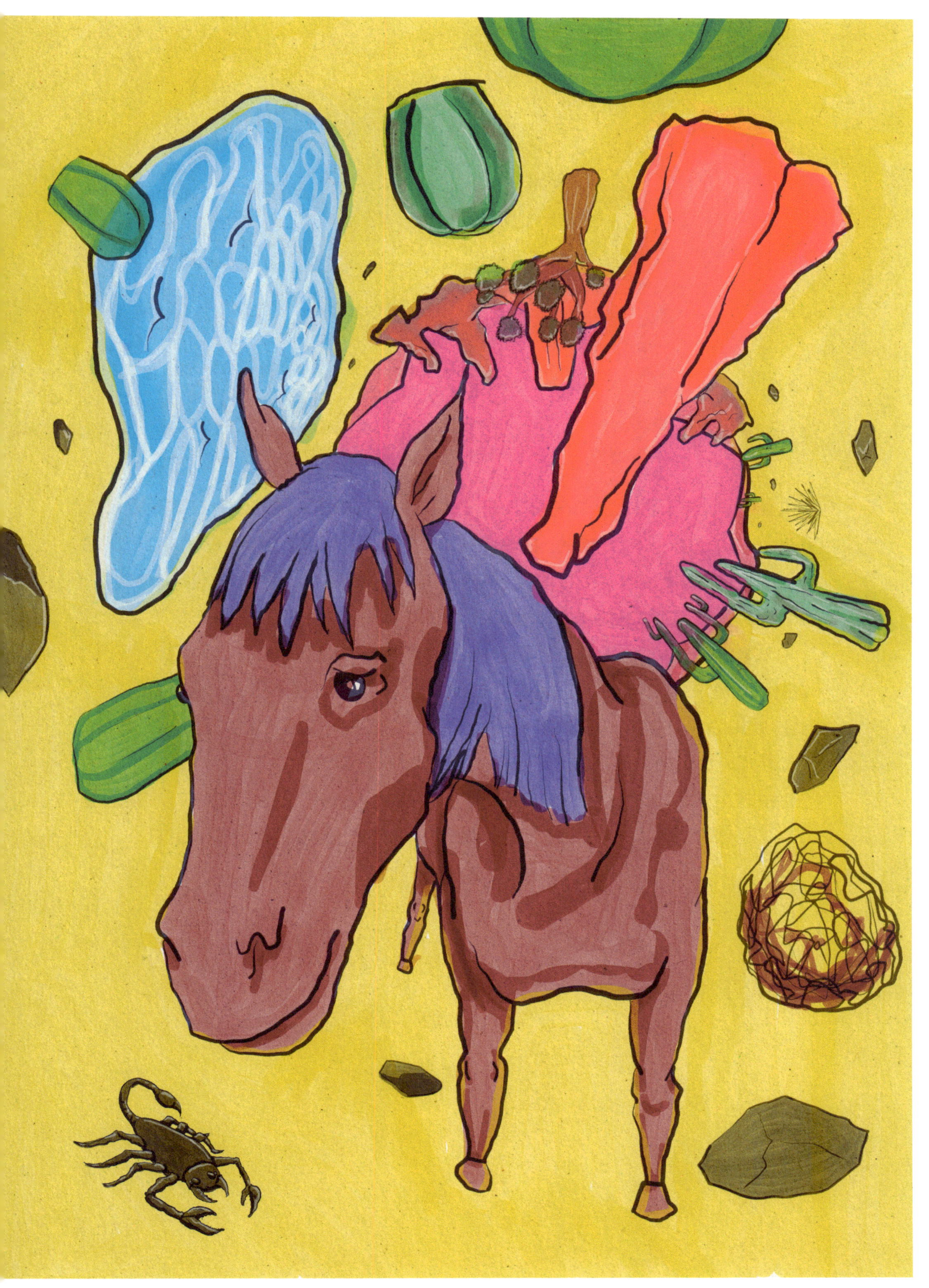

DAY XV
GUIDEBOOK

On Day 15, I hit a creative block—so I leaned into it and drew an open book, a simple yet fitting subject for the prompt. Sometimes, when the path forward feels unclear, books serve as guides, offering direction, knowledge, or just a moment of pause. This piece reflects that idea—an open book waiting to be filled with ideas, stories, or inspiration yet to come. In a way, it became a guide for my own creative journey, reminding me that even on days when the ideas don't flow easily, there's always a new page to turn.

DAY XVI
GRUNGY

For Day 16, I started an urban distortion piece, centering a Stratocaster guitar within a chaotic, rabbit hole-inspired perspective. Though unfinished, the composition leans into a raw, grungy aesthetic—where the city bends and warps around the instrument, mirroring the gritty, rebellious energy of rock music. The piece captures the feeling of sound ripping through space, much like the distorted chords of a grunge anthem. While I didn't complete it, the unfinished edges feel fitting, reinforcing the raw, unpolished nature of both the genre and the creative process itself.

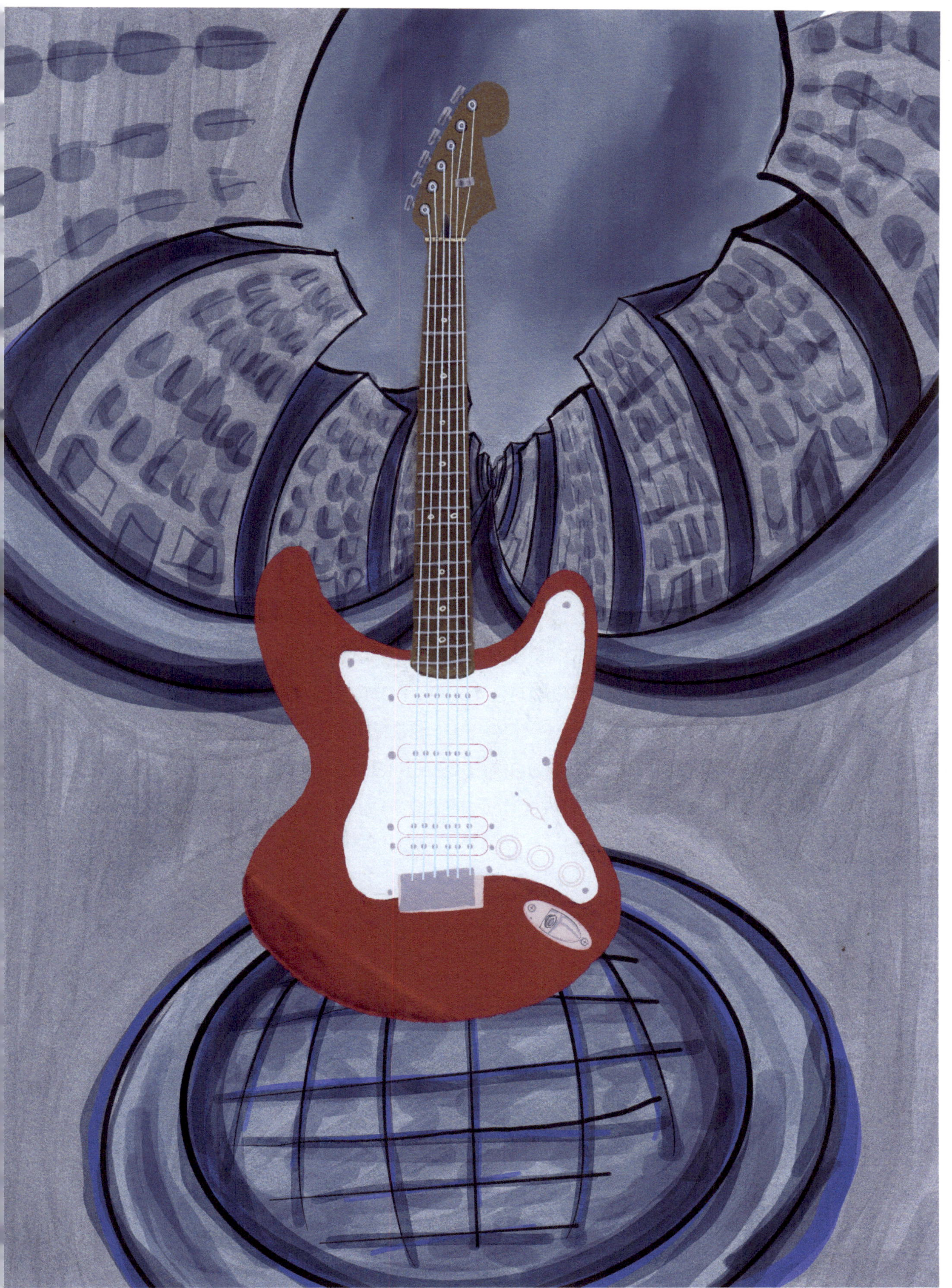

DAY XVII
JOURNAL

This piece was pure fun to create. Using my signature five-point perspective, I let looseleaf paper take center stage, floating and twisting through space in a dynamic, weightless composition. Each sheet feels like a fragment of thoughts, ideas, or stories caught mid-air—like a journal breaking free from its pages. The perspective enhances the sense of movement, giving the piece an almost dreamlike quality. This one felt like a celebration of creativity itself—the way ideas flow, scatter, and come together in unexpected ways.

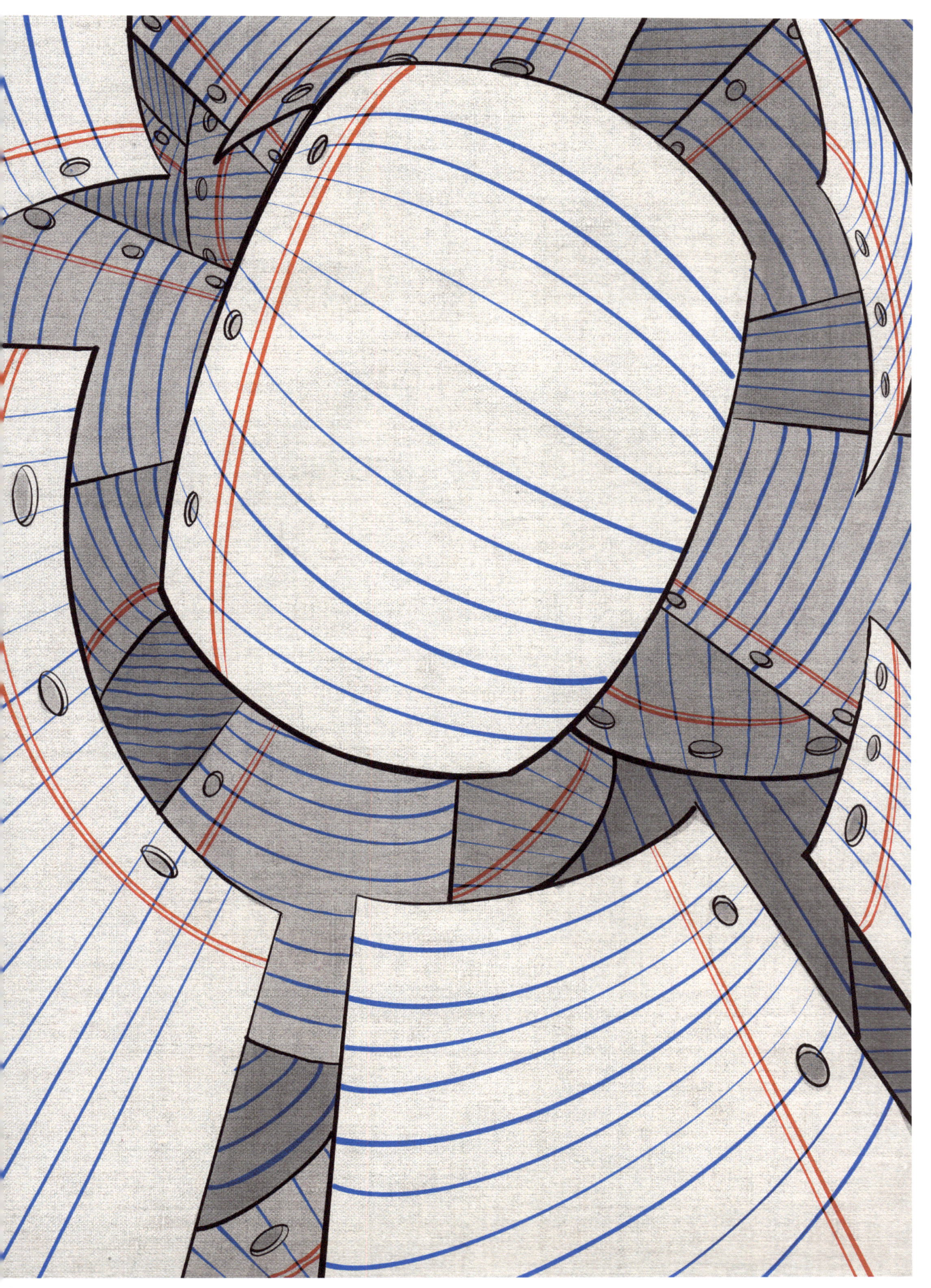

DAY XVIII
DRIVE

For Day 18, I brought my project car to life—my Honda with vertical doors and an Evo body kit—tearing through downtown Denver in a 5-point little planet perspective. The city wraps around the composition, creating a dynamic sense of motion, as if the car is driving through its own gravity-defying world. The exaggerated perspective enhances the energy of the piece, capturing the thrill of the open road and the love of modifying and personalizing a vehicle. This one was especially fun to draw, blending my passion for cars with my ongoing exploration of perspective.

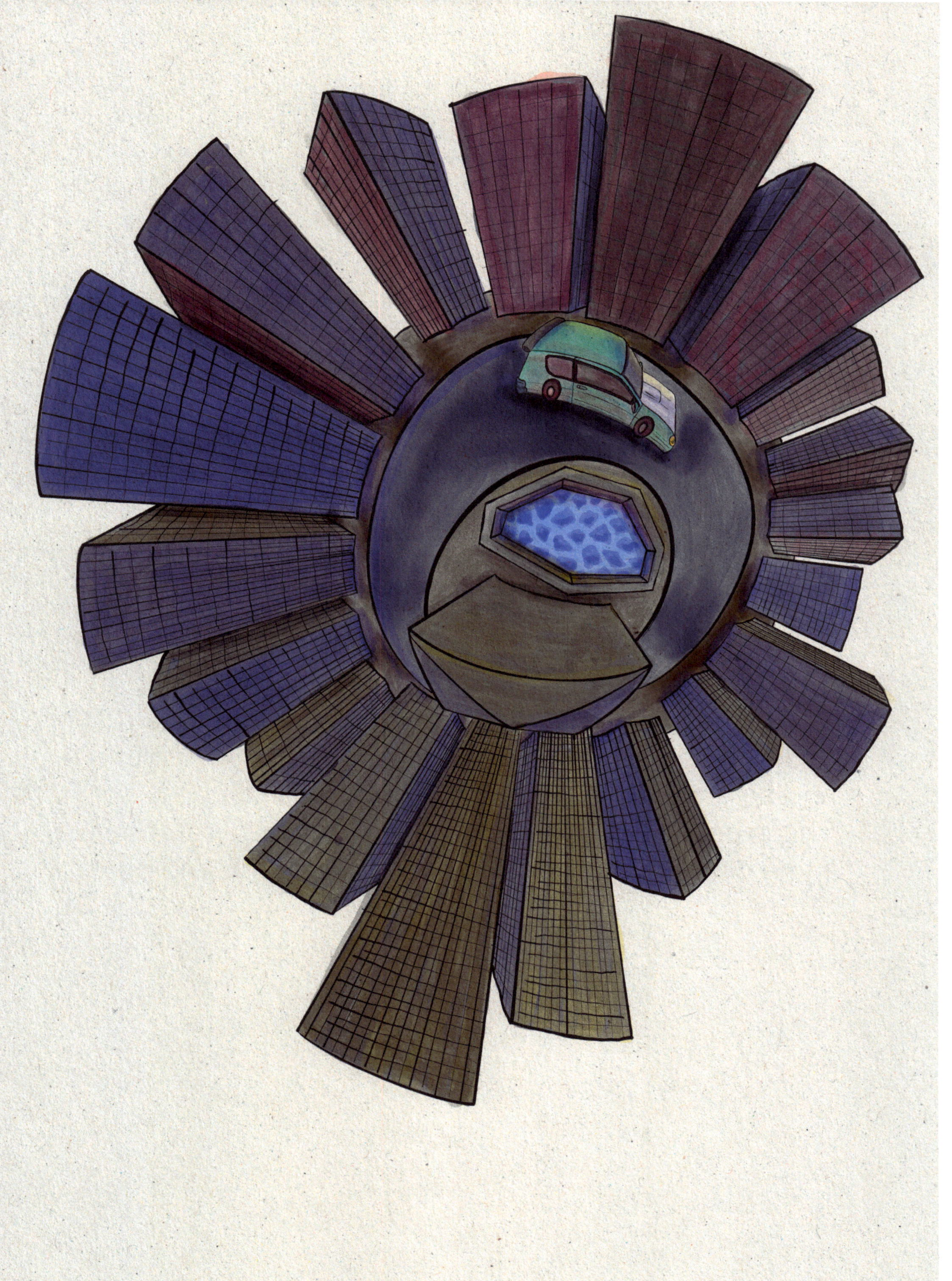

DAY XIX
RIDGE

For Day 19, I experimented with landscapes, creating a cliffside beach scene with a lighthouse overlooking the sea—framed within my signature 5-point little planet perspective. Using ink and markers, I focused on capturing the contrast between the rugged ridge, the vast ocean, and the guiding light of the lighthouse. The curved composition enhances the feeling of isolation and serenity, as if the scene exists within its own world. This piece was both a technical exercise in perspective and a chance to explore atmospheric depth and coastal textures.

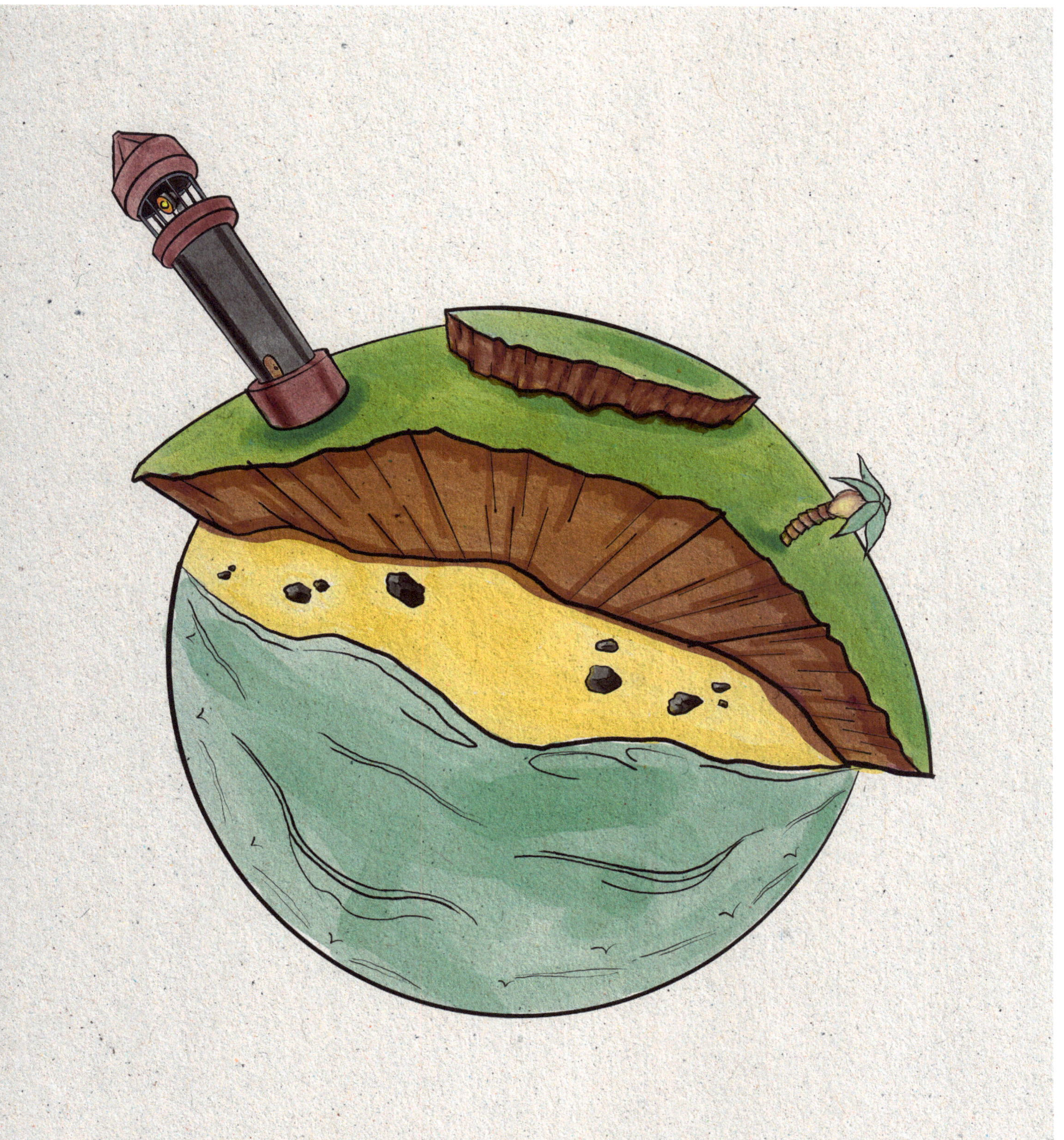

DAY XX
UNCHARTED

For Day 20, I ventured into the unknown, creating a vast, icy world—an ocean filled with towering glaciers, stretching into the blue expanse of an uncharted Antarctica. Using my signature 5-point perspective, I aimed to capture the raw, untouched beauty of the frozen landscape, where the horizon bends and disappears into the cold abyss. The interplay of ink and markers helped bring depth and contrast to the glacial forms, making the scene feel both expansive and isolated. This piece represents the thrill of exploration— stepping into worlds both real and imagined, where mystery and adventure await beyond every curve.

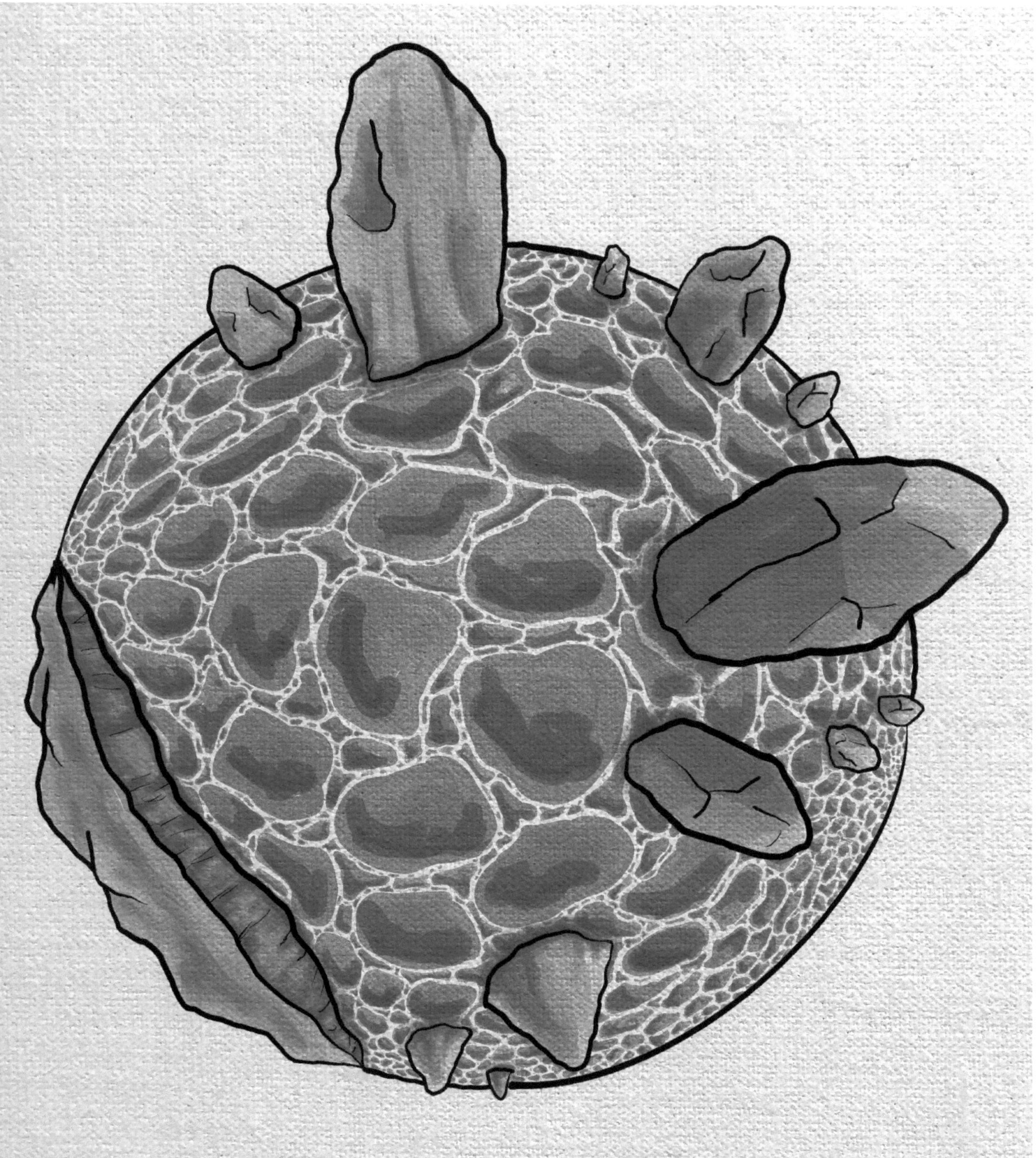

DAY XXI
RHINOCEROS

For Day 21, I played with scale and perspective, layering two interpretations of the theme within a 5-point little planet composition. A powerful rhinoceros stands on a beach, while a rhinoceros beetle appears close-up on a cliff—both creatures coexisting in the same surreal world. By blending earthy greens and browns with intricate layering, I aimed to create a sense of depth and contrast, emphasizing the vastness of nature and the similarities between these two vastly different creatures. This piece was an exploration of perspective beyond just space, but also in how we perceive size, importance, and connection in the natural world.

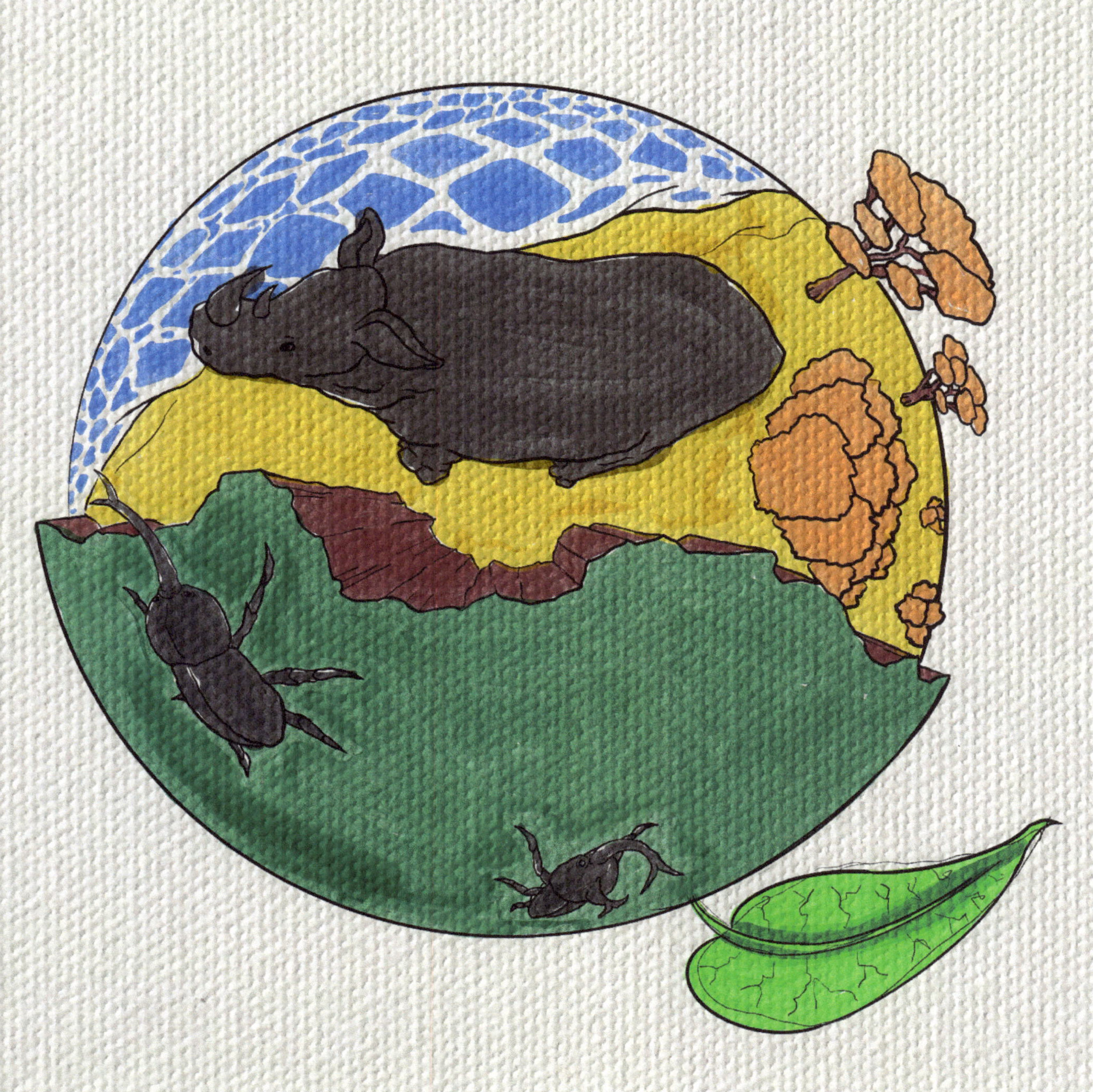

DAY XXII
CAMP

For Day 22, I took camping to an otherworldly level—
setting up a tent and campfire on the moon, all within a
5-point little planet perspective. The barren lunar
landscape curves around the composition, creating a
surreal yet peaceful sense of isolation. The idea of a
campfire burning in the vacuum of space adds a
playful, dreamlike contrast to the cold, desolate
environment. This piece blends adventure with
imagination, turning the moon into the ultimate
campsite, where the stars serve as both sky and ground
in an infinite cosmic expanse.

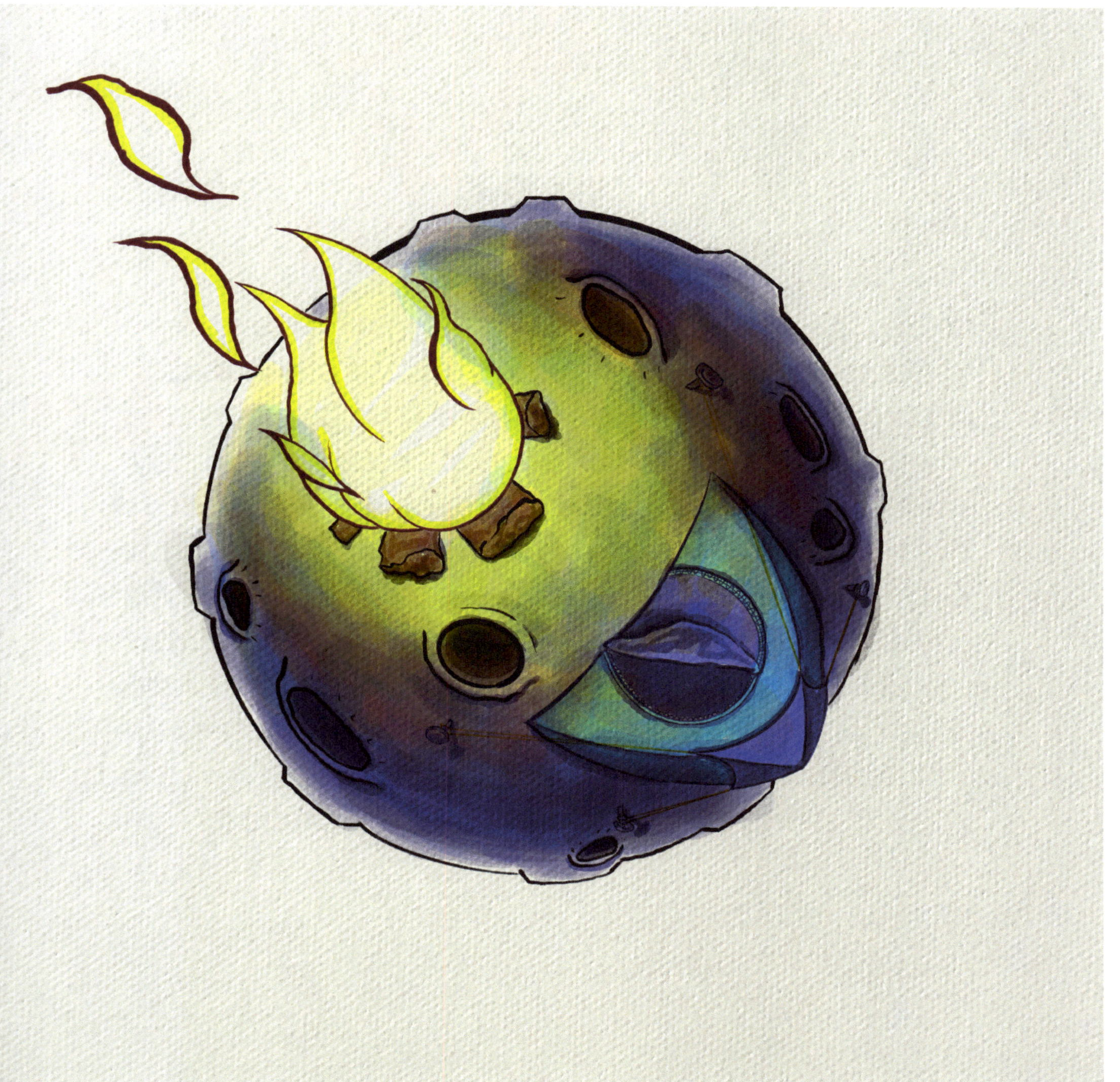

DAY XXIII
RUST

For Day 23, I set out to create a set of gears in 5-point perspective, aiming for an intricate mechanical composition. However, as I worked, I found myself a bit lost in the complexity of the forms and how they interacted within the curved space. The perspective didn't fully come out as planned, but the piece still carries the essence of decay and time—where rust creeps into once-perfect machinery, breaking down precision into something organic and unpredictable. Even when a drawing doesn't go as expected, the process itself becomes part of the journey, revealing lessons in form, depth, and adaptation.

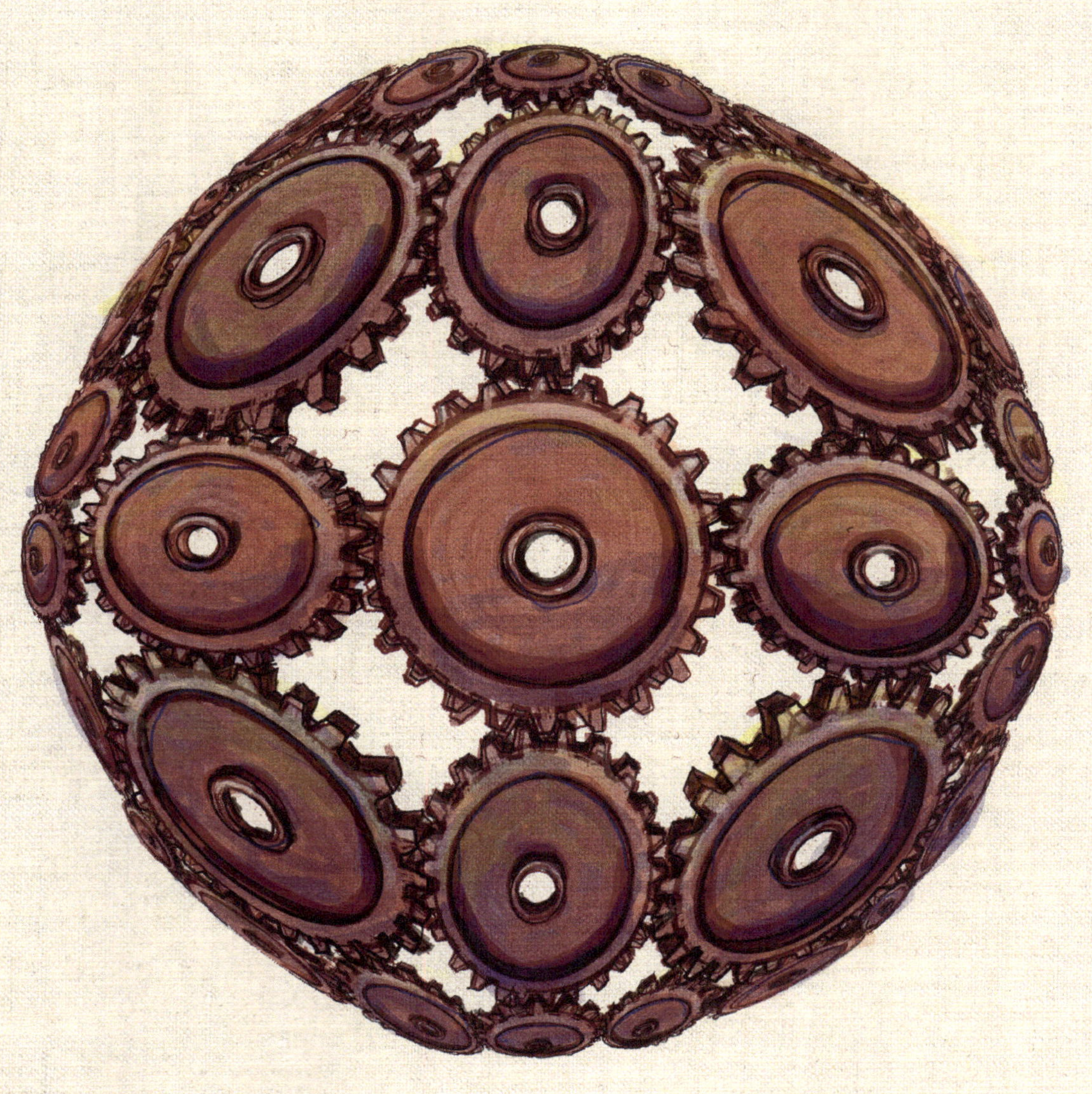

DAY XXIV
EXPEDITION

For Day 24, I expanded on my little planet 5-point perspective but zoomed in, immersing the viewer deep into a dense jungle inspired by *Indiana Jones*. The composition twists and curves, drawing the eye through tangled vines, towering trees, and ancient ruins hidden beneath the foliage. This piece was an adventure in itself—capturing the feeling of discovery, mystery, and the wild unknown. The closer perspective adds a new layer of depth to my ongoing exploration of curved space, making this expedition feel both intimate and boundless at the same time.

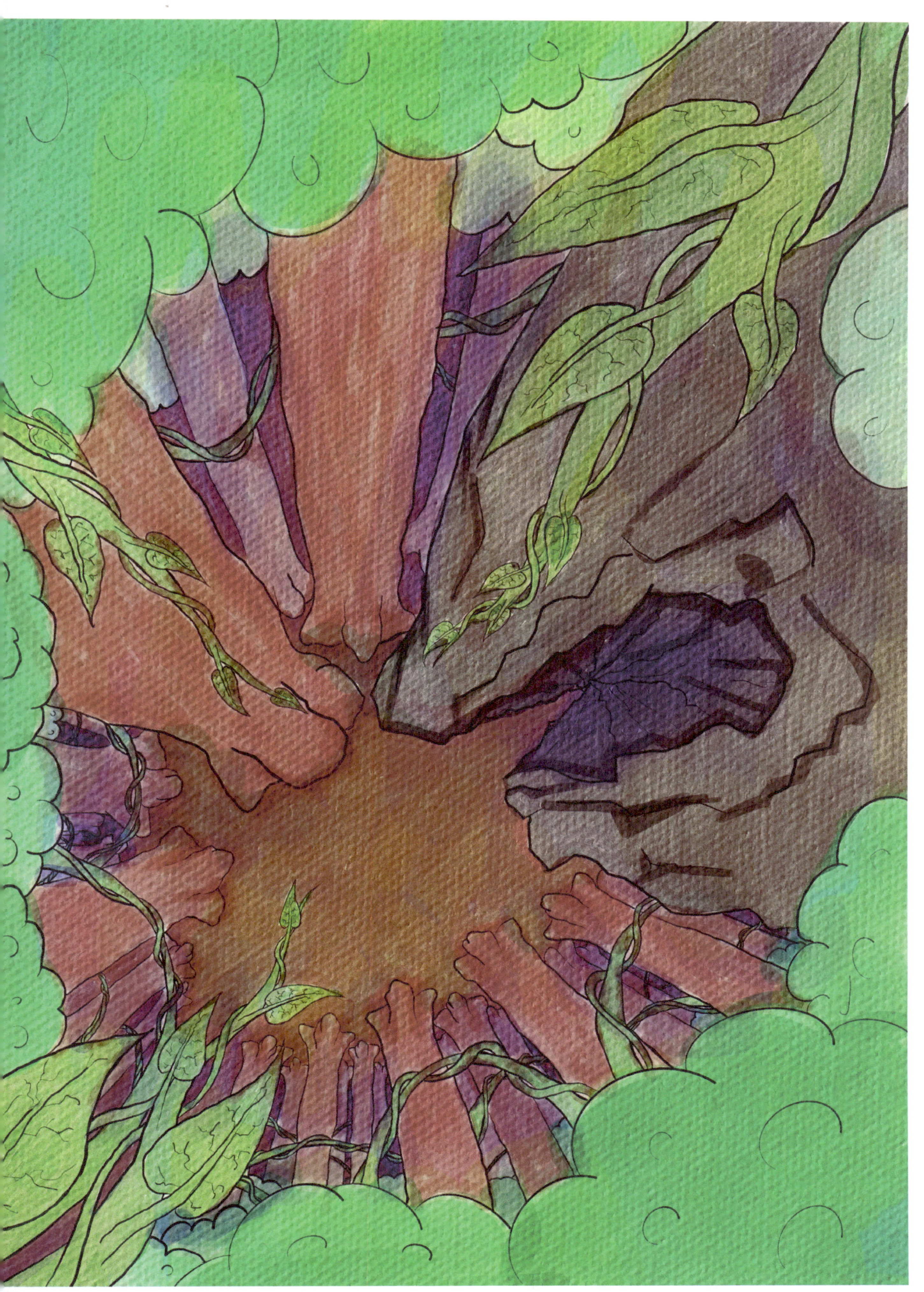

DAY XXV
SCARECROW

For Day 25, I embraced the autumn season with a 5-point little planet perspective, placing a lone scarecrow at the center of a vast farm ready for harvest. Pumpkins dot the landscape, curving around the world in a surreal yet cozy composition that captures the essence of fall. The warped perspective makes the fields feel endless, emphasizing the scarecrow's watchful presence over the land. This piece was a celebration of the season—of crisp air, golden fields, and the quiet guardians that stand among the crops as the harvest comes to an end.

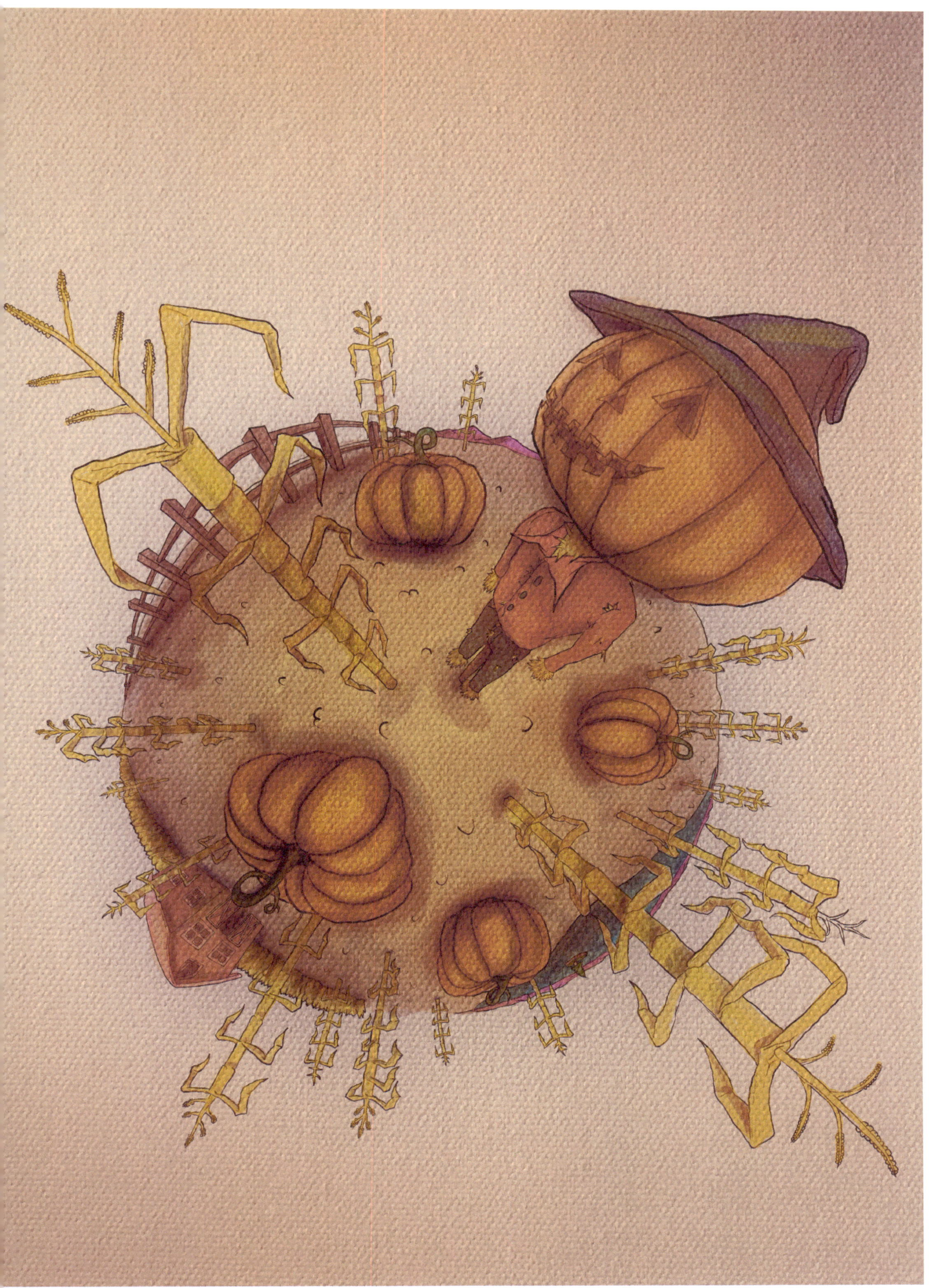

DAY XXVI
CAMERA

For Day 26, I played with perspective in a new way—drawing a flat camera but embedding a 5-point fisheye perspective within the reflection of its lens. The reflection warps and bends the world within, capturing the essence of how a camera distorts and frames reality. This piece became a study in duality—the structured, rigid form of the camera itself contrasted with the dynamic, curved space inside the lens. It's a reminder that what we see is often shaped by the tools we use to capture it, and perspective is always a matter of how we choose to frame the world around us.

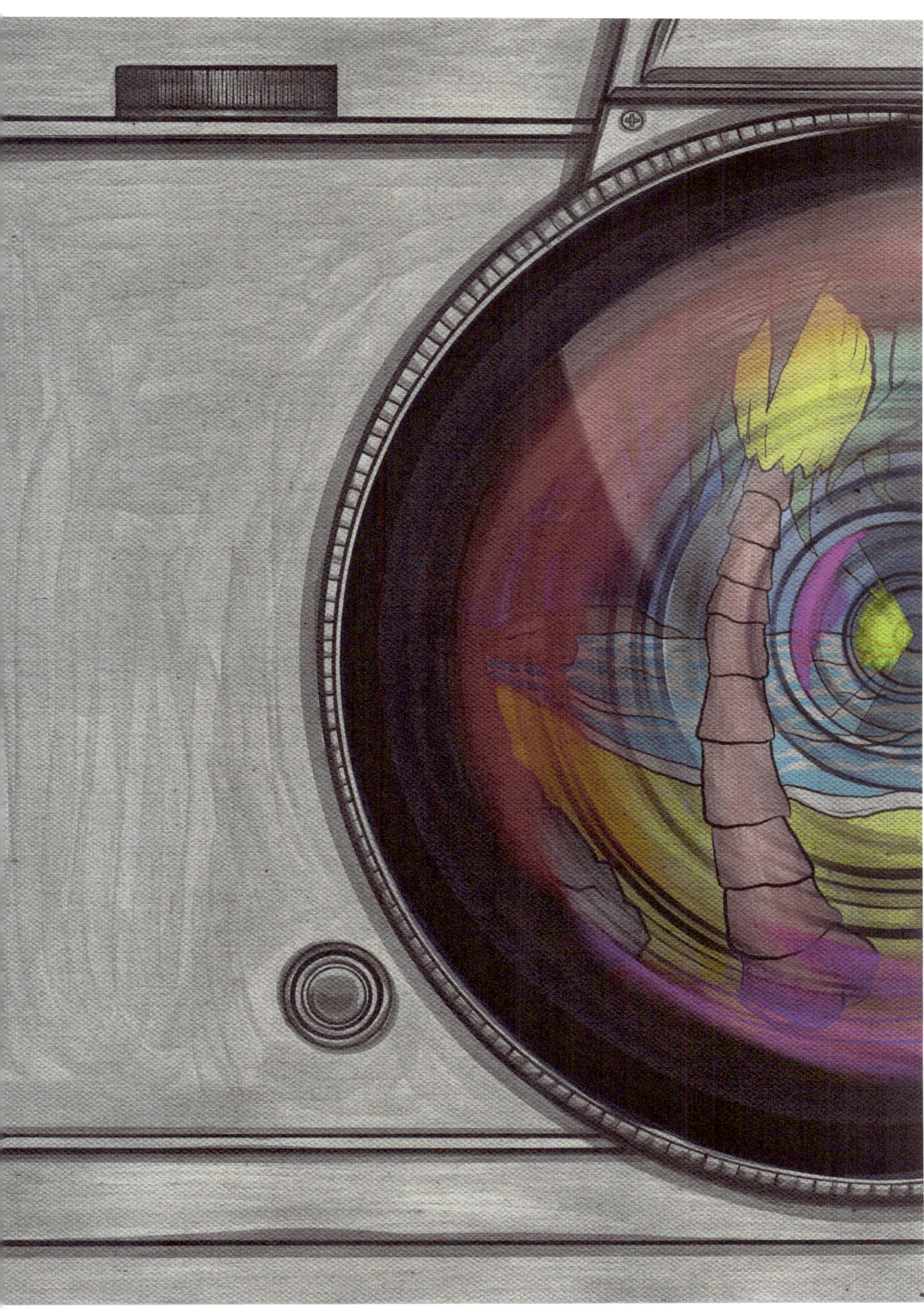

DAY XXVII
ROAD

For Day 27, I experimented with dual 5-point perspectives, almost forming two separate planets that merge into a single road. This piece plays with symmetry and reflection, creating a surreal, mirrored world where two perspectives meet at the horizon. The road becomes the connection between these distorted realities, guiding the eye through the warped landscape. This was an exciting challenge in perspective, pushing the limits of depth and composition while reinforcing the idea that all paths, no matter how different, eventually lead somewhere.

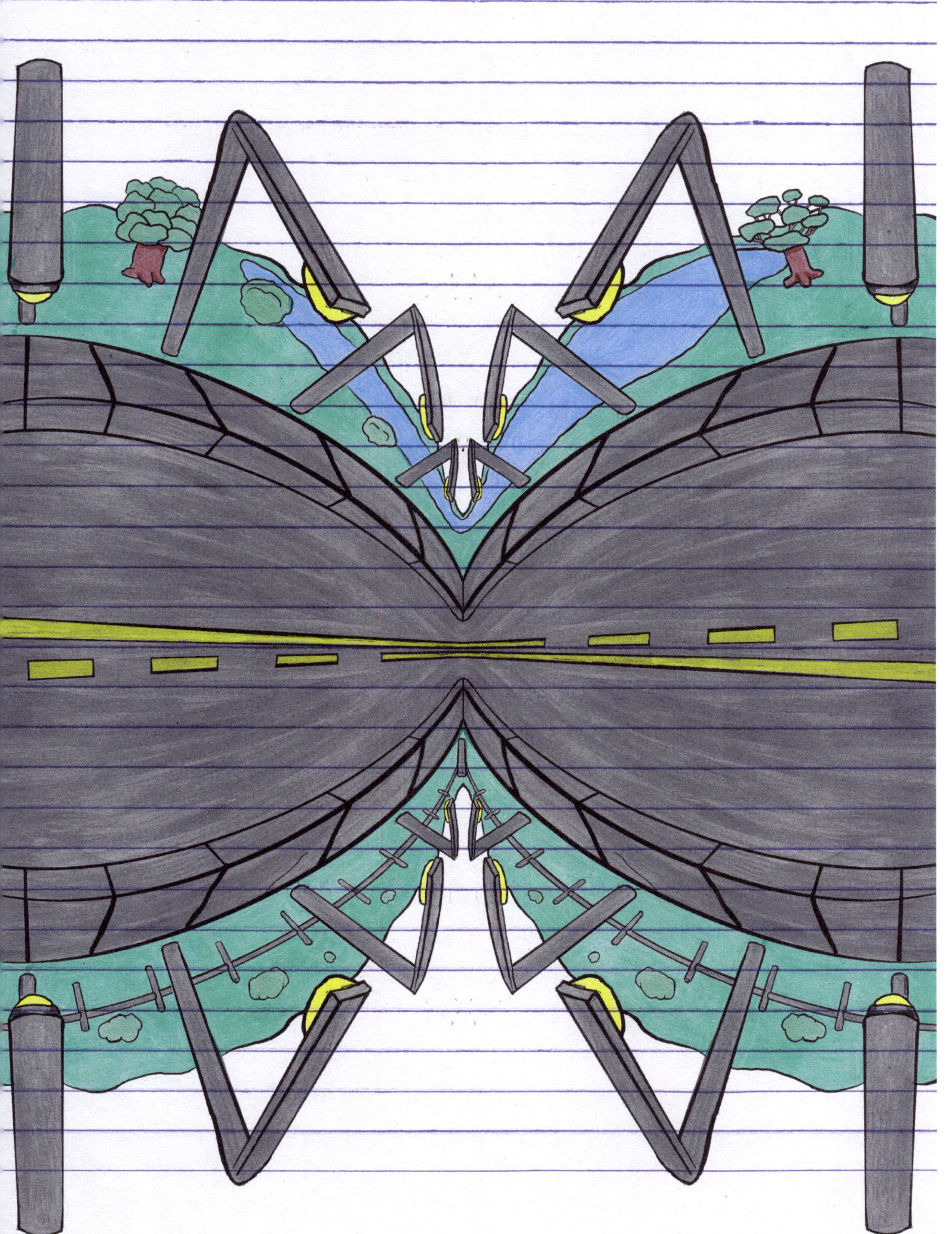

DAY XXVIII
JUMBO

For Day 28, I returned to my 5-point little planet perspective, this time bringing together two massive creatures in an unexpected setting—an elephant and a giant squid on an African beach. The exaggerated curvature of the landscape enhances the surreal contrast between land and sea, as if these titans of different worlds have crossed paths in a dreamlike meeting. This piece was an exploration of scale and balance, using perspective to unite the natural and the fantastical in a single, immersive composition.

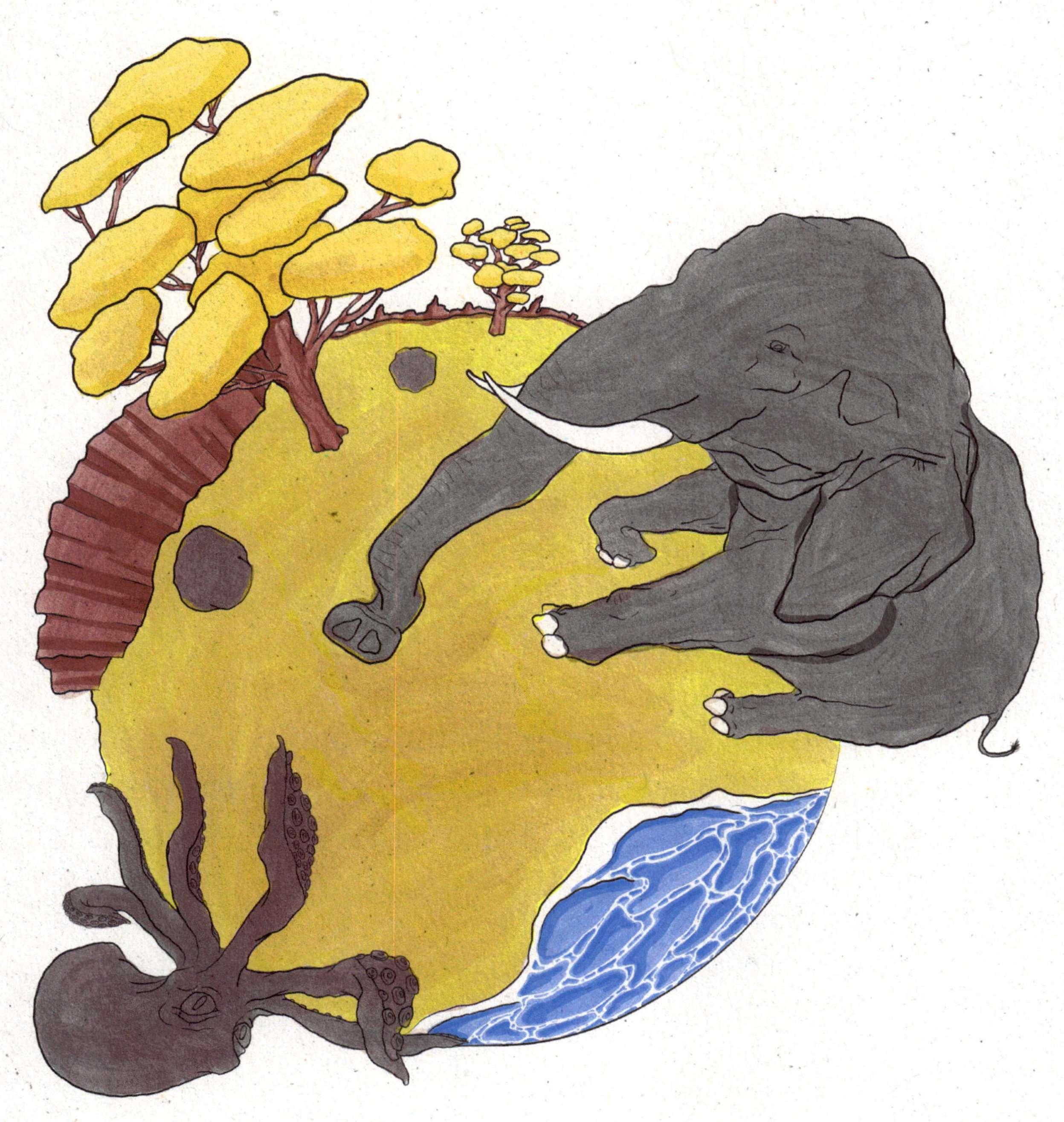

DAY XXIX
NAVIGATOR

For Day 29, I took inspiration from the winding waterways of Louisiana, illustrating an alligator navigating the bayous. Using my signature 5-point perspective, I aimed to capture the slow, stealthy movement of this ancient predator as it glides through the murky waters, surrounded by dense cypress trees and tangled roots. The curved composition enhances the sense of direction and flow, making the alligator feel like the true master of its domain. This piece embodies patience, precision, and the quiet confidence of a natural-born navigator.

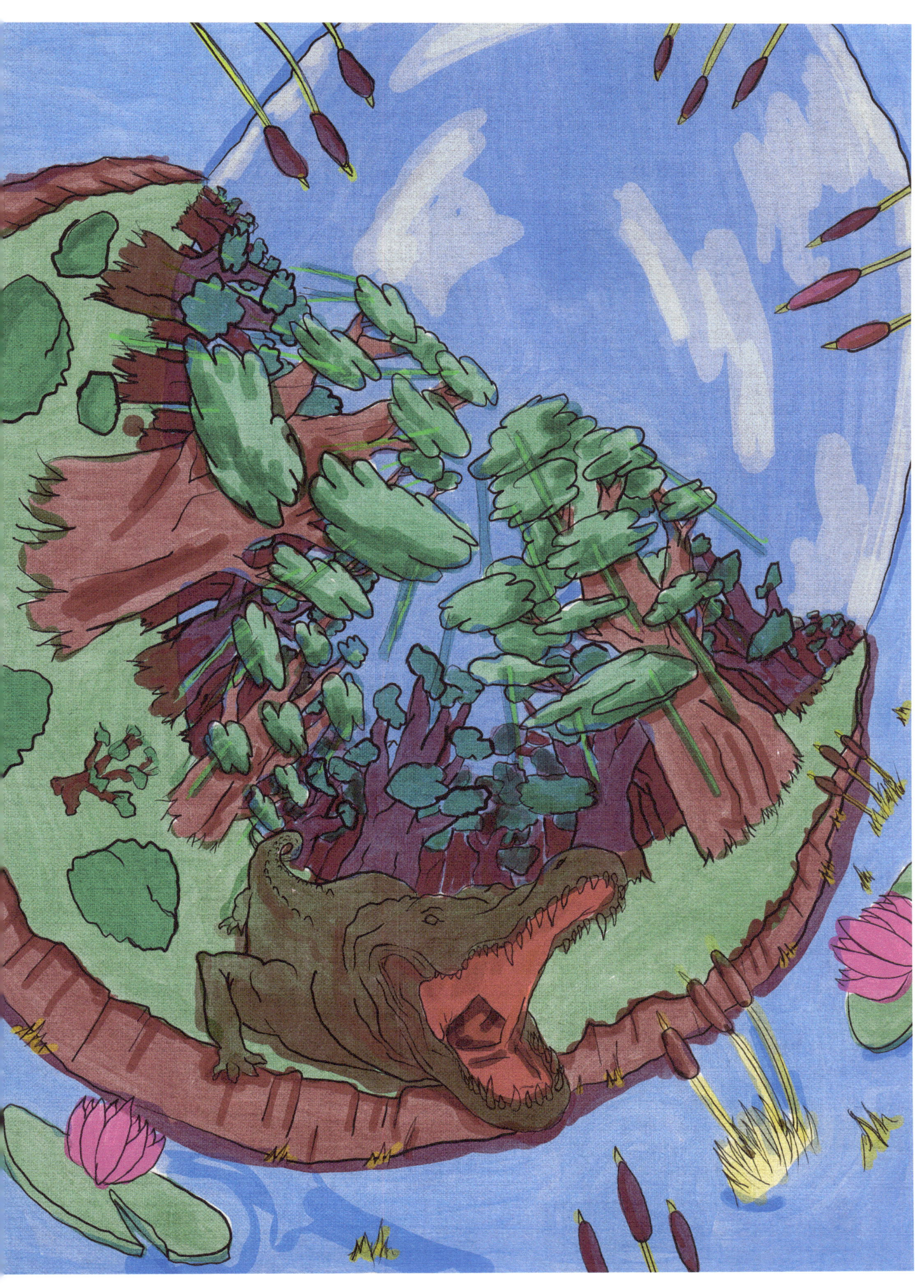

DAY XXX
VIOLIN

For Day 30, I returned to the rabbit hole perspective I explored in Days 10 and 14, this time bringing a whimsical twist—placing a squirrel at the center stage of an opera house, playing a violin. The dramatic, spiraling perspective adds to the theatrical energy of the composition, making the performance feel grand and immersive. This piece was a playful fusion of elegance and charm, combining the refined world of classical music with the lively spirit of nature. It was a fun way to push the limits of perspective while celebrating the power of storytelling through art.

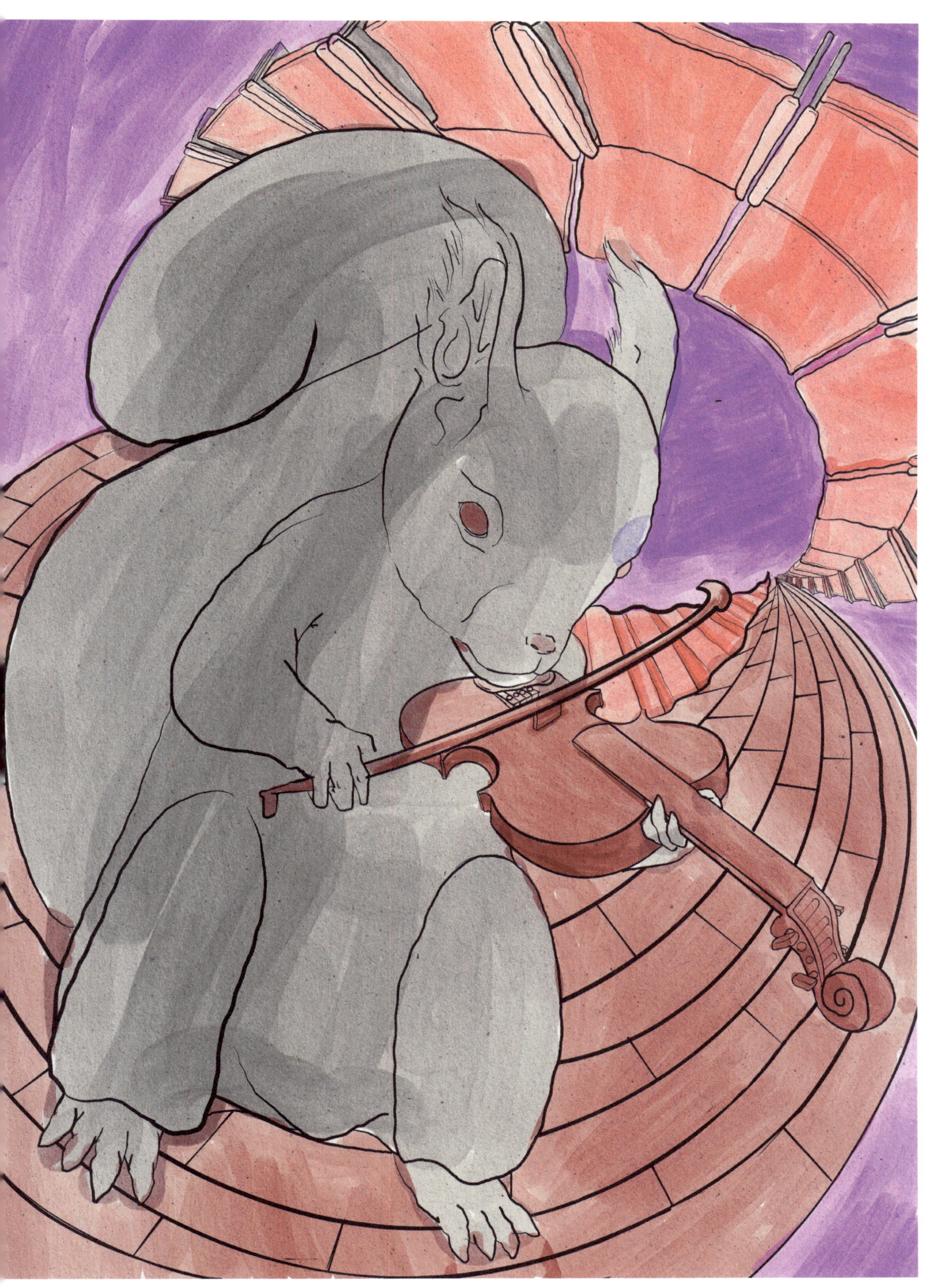

DAY XXXI
LANDMARK

For the grand finale of Inktober, I chose one of my favorite cities—Seattle—focusing on the iconic Space Needle through my signature rabbit hole perspective. The towering landmark stretches into the spiraling composition, surrounded by the city's skyline as if being pulled into its own gravitational field. This piece was a fitting way to close out the challenge, combining my love for architecture, perspective, and dynamic storytelling in a single, immersive drawing. It encapsulates the essence of exploration, both in art and in the world itself, making it the perfect landmark to end this creative journey.

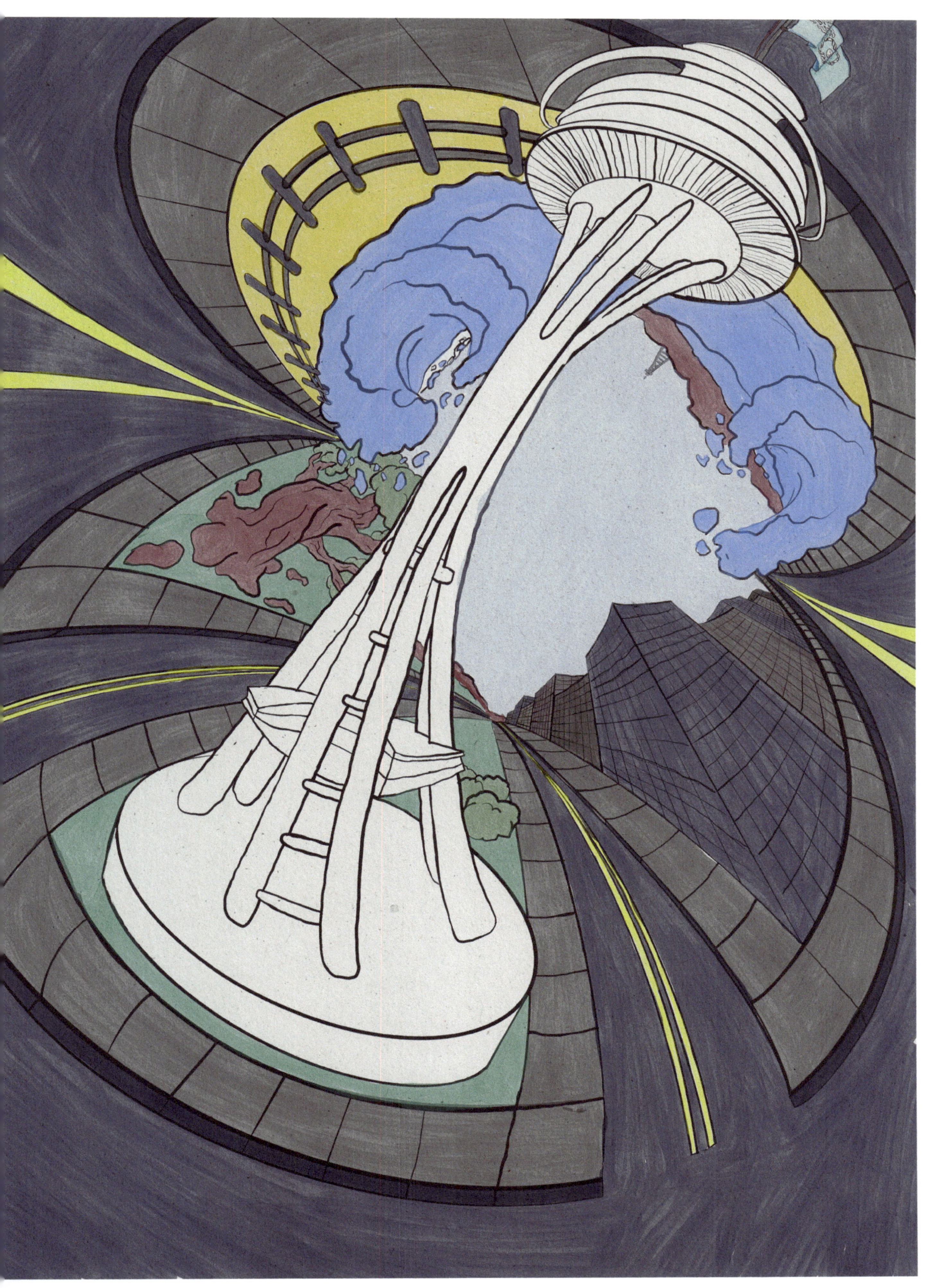

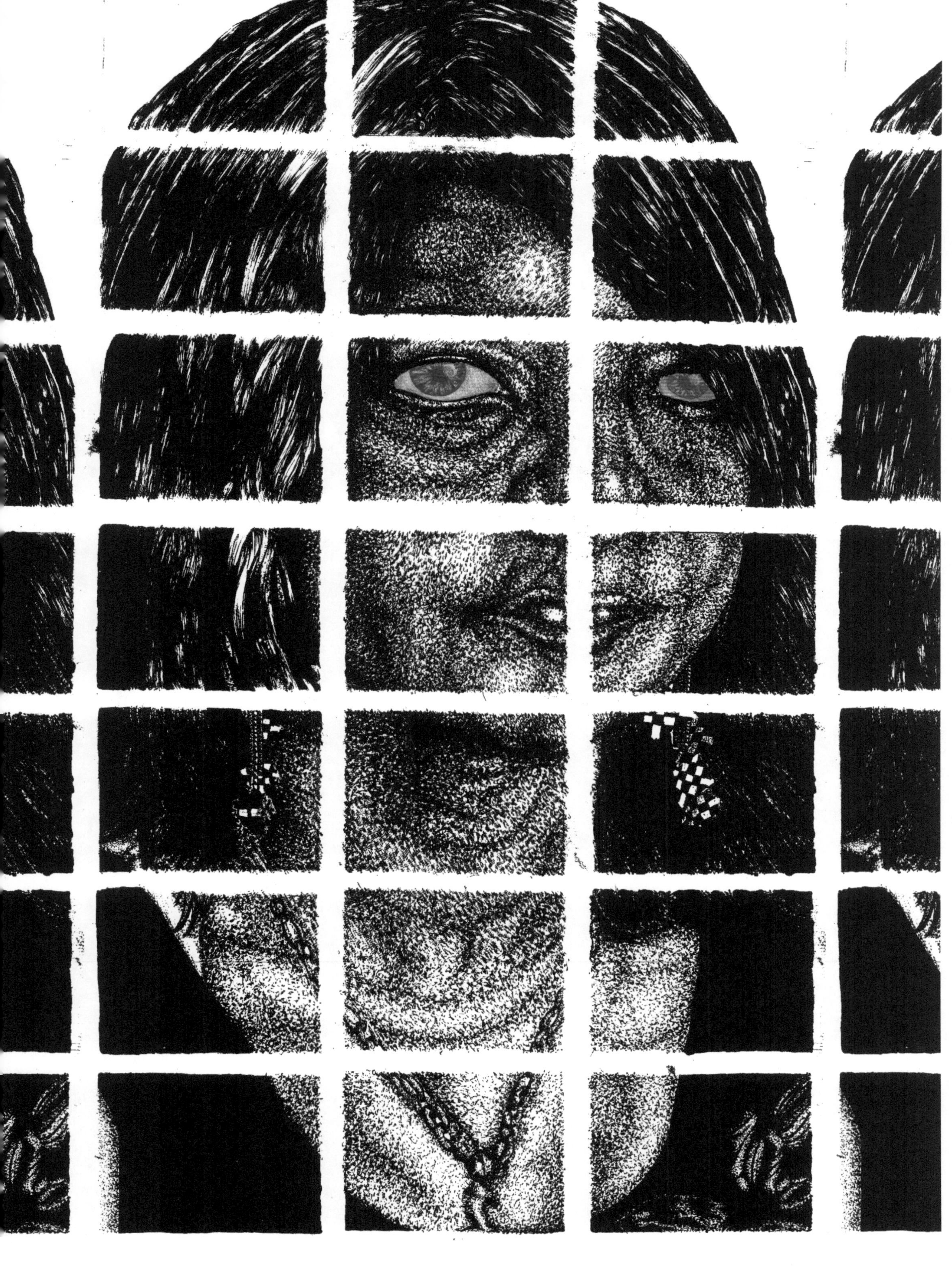

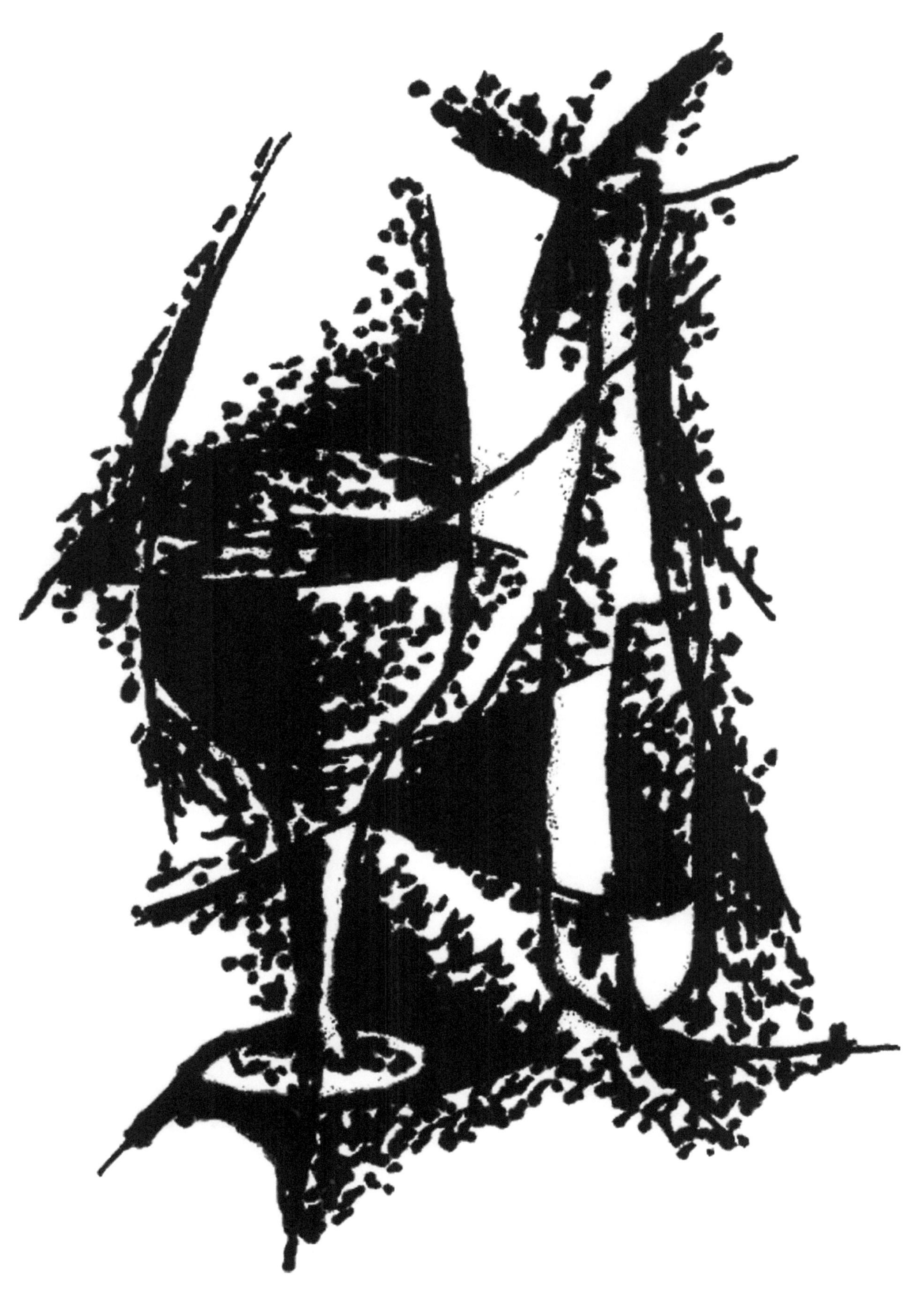

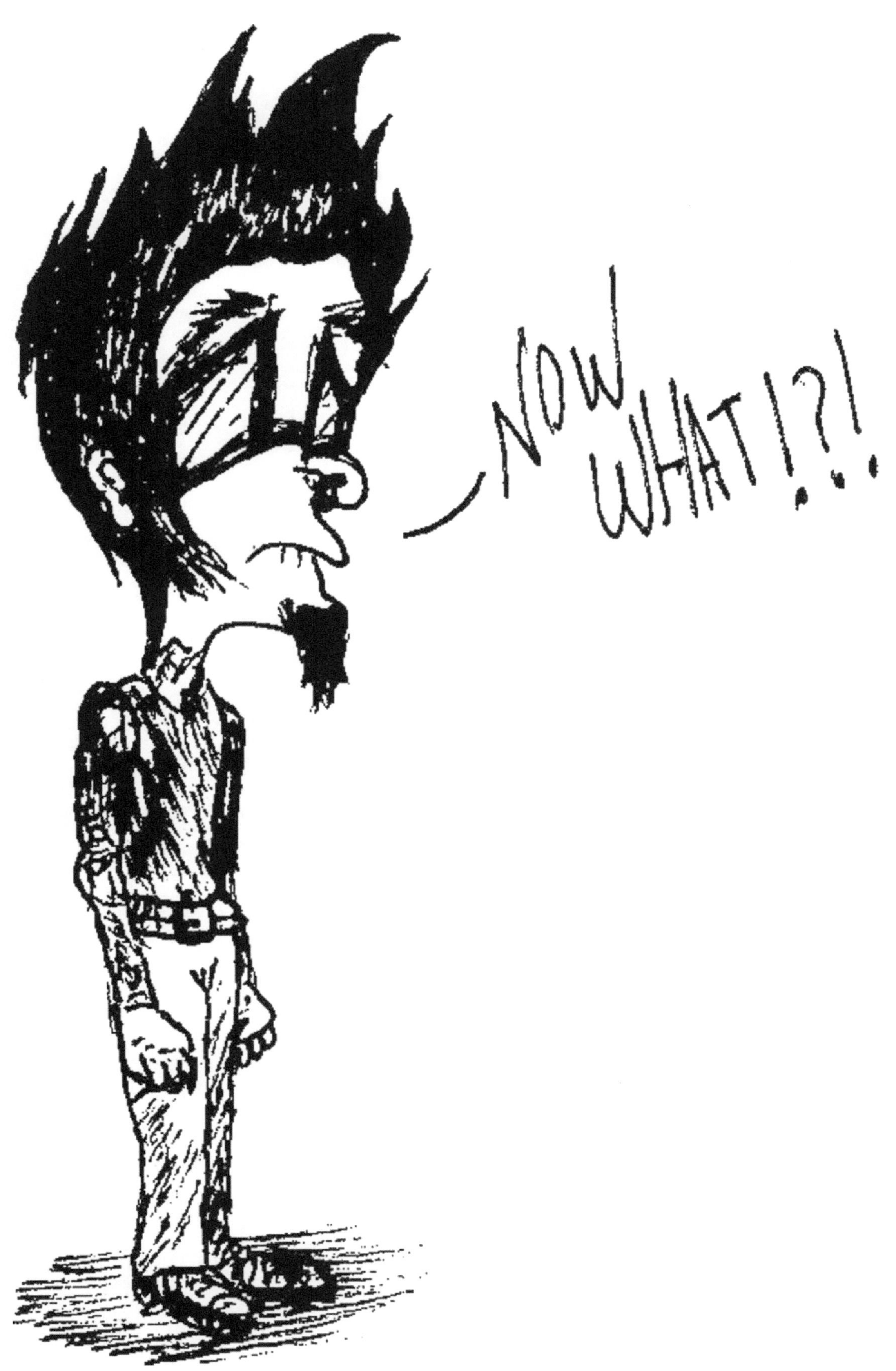

NOW
WHAT!?!

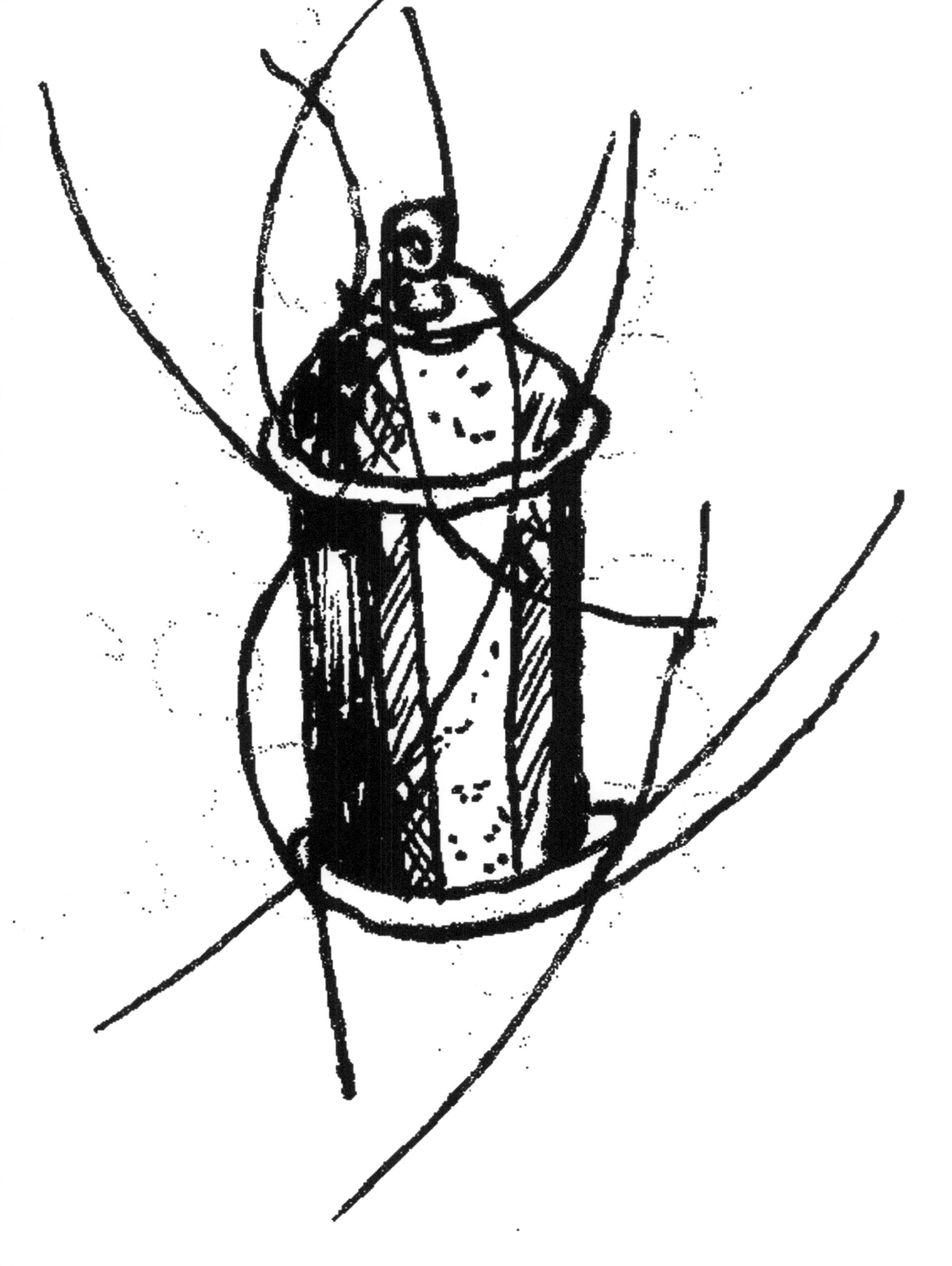

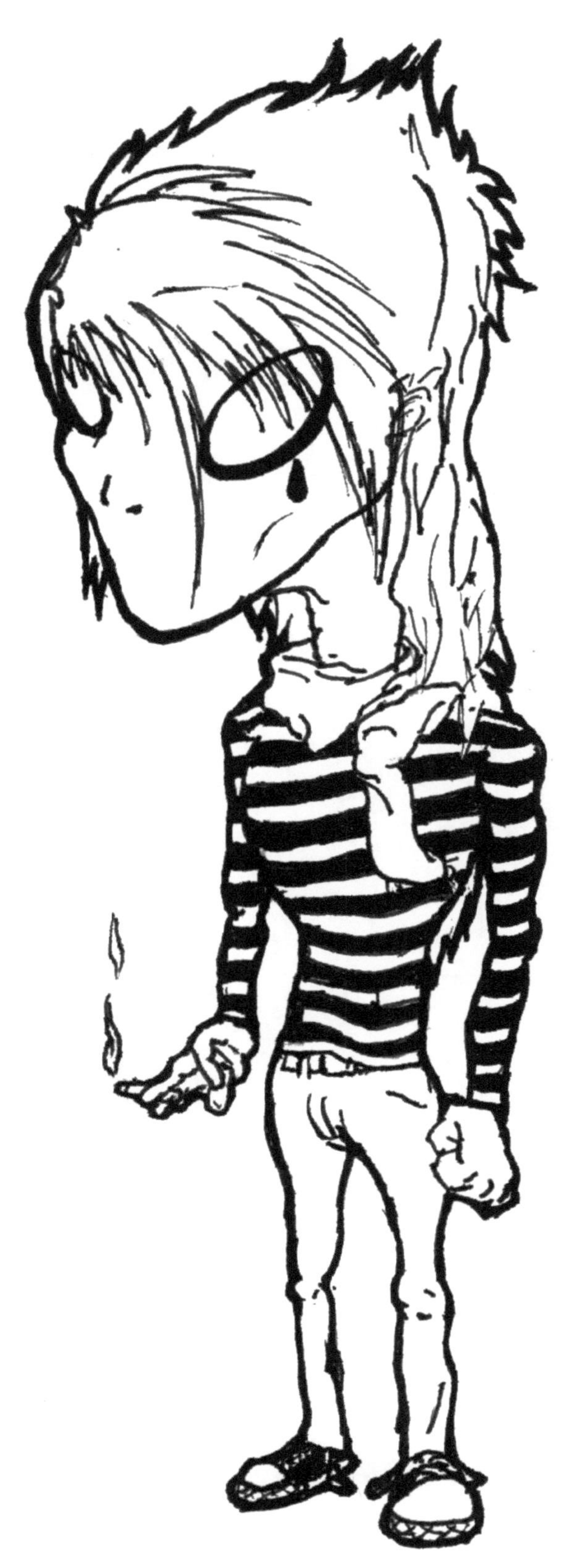

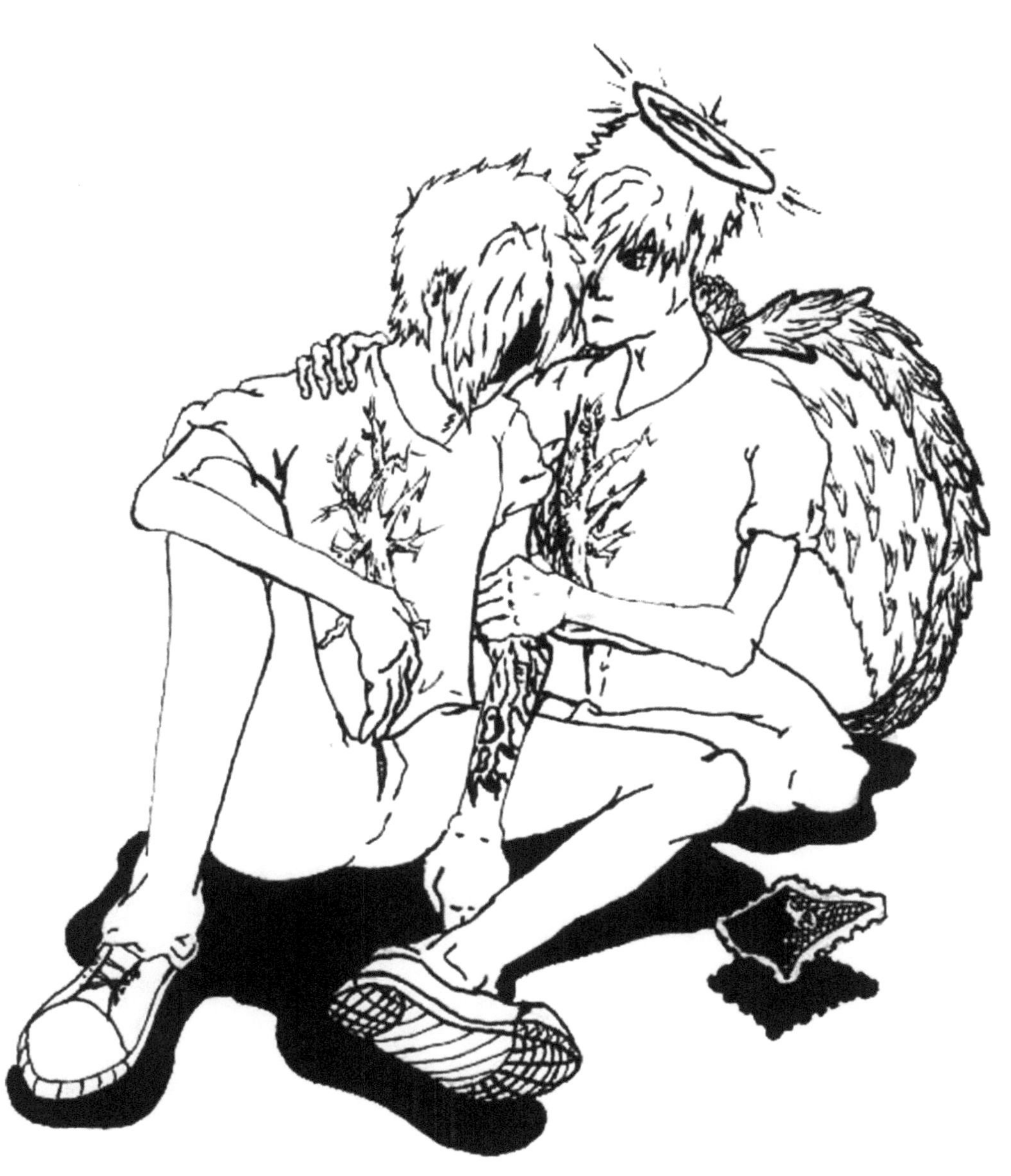